AN INCREDIBLE JOURNEY

*The Living Event of Human Life from Pre-Existence
to Reincarnation to the Ascensional Way*

E MESTRAUD

This book is intended as the first in a series of esoteric works around this and other topics.

AN INCREDIBLE JOURNEY : THE LIVING EVENT OF THE HUMAN LIFE

Copyright © 2023 E Mestraud.

All rights reserved. Printed in the United Kingdom. No part of this book may be used or reproduced in any manner whatsoever without written permission except in the case of brief quotations em- bodied in critical articles or reviews.

For information contact **http://www.virsel.com**

ISBN: 9798869886620

First Edition : December 2023

10 9 8 7 6 5 4 3 2 1

Table of Contents

A PRELUDE 1

PREFACE 2

INTRODUCTION 6

CHAPTER 1: NUMBER 1 14

CHAPTER 2: PRE LIFE SETTINGS 36

CHAPTER 3: THE EVENT OF TERM OF PREGNANCY- STAGE THREE 63

CHAPTER 4: FIRST PHYSICAL LIFE 82

CHAPTER 5: STAGE 5 AFTERLIFE STAGE 2 107

CHAPTER 6: COLUMN 6: THE SECOND PHYSICAL LIFE 126

CHAPTER 7: 2ND AFTERLIFE SETTINGS (STAGE 7) 139

CHAPTER 8: (STAGE 8) THIRD PHYSICAL LIFE 156

CHAPTER 9: 3RD AFTER-LIFE SETTINGS 174

CHAPTER 10: FIRST THEREAFTER EVENT 189

APPENDIX I 208

.... 211

APPENDIX II 212

Dedication

This Work is dedicated to those who, throughout the millennia, have worked tirelessly for Actuality, Truth and the Evolution of the Living Human Event.

A Prelude

Before approaching the Book, the reader is advised that this is very new information and the language and terms of reference in it is used in a very particular way which most people will be unfamiliar with. For this reason, the writer has provided a Glossary of the key terms used together with the relevant charts at the back of the book. The reader is advised to make good use of this as it will make the contents of the Book clearer and easier to grasp.

Preface

Origins of this Work

THIS BOOK ROSE AS A CONSEQUENCE of an esoteric Work of Life that has been in process for many years. The people involved were not satisfied with what is generally available in the world as a foundation for living and determined to find a way that satisfied a hunger for something real. As a consequence, they looked for something that does not rely upon belief or faith but on the evidence of the natural Laws that govern all life here. Central to the work is a determination to be fully oneself, a unique individual with unique passions and abilities and to pursue that quest in every way

PREFACE

possible, if necessary, in defiance of cultural imperatives (meaning the ways in which twenty-first century makes demands on our time).

Alongside the quest to become fully ourselves came a determination to base our work on the natural ways of the Planet and the Solar System, as it was recognised that the way ahead could only be secured and guaranteed if it could be measured against an, unbiased criteria which was not susceptible to human persuasion. Clearly, the planet is a great web of inter-connected life that aims at harmony and balance and we ourselves are a part of that. Obviously, a person has to start from the actuality of where they are, no point in trying to begin at the other end of creation.

Once begun, the work snowballed and delivered up a wealth of understanding of the natural laws, human history and the need to develop and change; at the same time, we found ourselves to be more and more in touch with what we felt to be the real self. In recent years the work has opened up to great revelations regarding not just the origins of life but the afterlife and the greater promise of being human. This is the substance of this book; the reader may choose to regard it as a philosophical argument but for us, having done the work of it, it is very real.

Consequently, we decided to write this book primarily for people who are looking for the answers to the big questions......questions like why am I here, where did I come from, what happens to me after the death of my physical body, is there a purpose for living beyond what is currently understood by today's culture?

The book is part of an entirely new kind of science, rarely hinted at and never previously explained. It is something we all felt was desperately needed in an increasingly complex world in which more and more people appear to feel lost and overwhelmed – which is probably why so many are fascinated by the natural worlds which instinctively draw us to our origins.

The need to understand our origins and the reasons for our existence is what drew us collectively to this work in the first place.

Our intention originally was to present people with a deeper understanding of the Actuality of Reincarnation and the mechanics by which it occurs (because the work we engage in starts with the premise that although faith and belief are important props in life it should be possible to find logistical proof for a subject within the natural laws if that subject is REAL).

However, it rapidly became clear that limiting the book to solely Reincarnation would deprive the reader of the much bigger picture that everyone needs to locate their life and as a consequence the afterlife chart (found at the back of the book) was created and provides the framework for the book.

Certainly, reincarnation is a useful starting point for many people because it is the 'modus operandi' for so many faiths but for us it is only a small part of the picture. Any comprehensive enquiry into the human situation needs to begin outside the local conditions of life (planetary) and embrace creational purpose, because after many years of research we have concluded that all is inter-related; the Planet is dependent on the Sun and other planets within the Solar System, the Sun is a part of our galaxy, which is part of the super- cluster Laniakia (of which the Milky Way is only a small part) and so on. Nothing exists as an independent nodule any more than a person's little toe can exist independently from their entire body. For this reason, the book starts with the bigger picture, the

PREFACE

making of life in Creation and its journey through Creation prior to its appearance here, on the Planet. It is not within the scope of this book to prove to the reader that this is more than a working hypothesis (as for us it is the upshot of many dedicated years of work that it is quite impossible to bottom line). We therefore offer it as a "philosophy" which the reader is quite at liberty to dispute having examined the work for themselves.

Introduction

MOST PEOPLE HAVE HEARD OF REINCARNATION and there are millions of people who embrace it as an article of faith. Equally, many people instinctively feel that there is more to life than is currently on offer and have an inner knowing that nudges them towards a deeper exploration of the meaning of life. For those who care to investigate there is a wealth of phenomena – inexplicable early childhood memories, déjà vu, children who insist they were someone else previously, even a powerful fascination with a different culture or period in history which add weight and substance to these beliefs. In addition, we live on a planet where re-occurrence – the continual recycling of the seasons, the carbon cycle (in which an atom of carbon may be in a plant one day, be eaten by a cow the next, be eaten by a human the day after, ending up as a part of the body the next, then be breathed out by the human to become part of the air, only then to be once more taken up by a plant), even the way we see friends repeat the same mistakes in their relationships – is the order of the day. Given all this, a person of vision and imagination, considering the many possibilities that exist here, might look at a newly-dug grave and wonder, looking at the surrounding churchyard, how many other graves that life might already have occupied?

This book explores not just the actuality of reincarnation but opens the doors of perception and understanding to a much bigger picture; many people have speculated and wondered about the possibility of an afterlife – and religion and philosophy have mused about this for millennia, creating their own dogma alongside it – but very few seem to have considered what might be the case pre-conception. This is a unique and far-reaching exploration of the human event, its origins and its possibility, which does stretch beyond reincarnation, even though reincarnation and the afterlife is an important feature of it. Most importantly, it asks the question how does this affect you and what does it mean for your life?

Everyone can agree that the human race has made a long historical journey that culminates in these times but equally each individual person is making a journey, which others see only a snapshot of, not realising that that journey may have started in the distant past and may stretch forward in time to a very different future. And indeed, some may have no previous journey to speak of but are maybe setting out now for the first time, with all to discover and win for themselves.

The book clearly begins with the premise that life exists beyond the physical and that there is a (mostly) unseen world that nonetheless is very real and which in actuality drives our existence here. There is a wealth of evidence that the human today does not have total perception of the actuality of life; firstly, humans are limited by the physical attributes of the body (no one will ever run a mile in a minute without artificial assistance) and secondly, in their current state of evolution they cannot see the range of colours that, as an example, bees see. Neither can their sense of smell or hearing compete with that of a dog. So, it is not unreasonable to suggest that there is a wealth of phenomena and experience available beyond that of the physical world and indeed, sensitive people throughout the ages have spoken and written about it. Much of the so-called mystical experiences of humans in past times, as an example the sight of the halo or a bright glow around human life can be attributed to a momentary glimpse of the unseen worlds and of course there have been a multitude of people, from Nostradamus to Madame Blavatsky who seem to have had divinatory abilities. A brief glance at history shows that over the millennia, and particularly since the advent of the Industrial Revolution, humans have lost many natural abilities, such as the ability to see auras, to be divinatory, to sense atmospheres and so much more. Perhaps this is not the case with so-called primitive peoples, such as the Aborigines and certain Amazon tribes, and it is certainly not the case with animal life which still retains its natural connections to the planet (as a consequence, animals instinctively flee an area which is about to suffer devastation from an earthquake whilst humans carry on regardless) but it is very much the situation of the modern human. Nonetheless, even today, many people instinctively sense when there is bad feeling or an "atmosphere" in a room, even though they can't rationalise or explain it and many will quickly cotton on to the fact that a couple have just had an argument no matter how hard they try to hide it! And on a brighter note, many people will know older couples who know in advance what each other are thinking and pre-empt each other's needs!

PREFACE

At the same time, our experience of life should teach us that, if there is an unseen world, it unquestionably contains a vast range of different qualities ranging from very fine to very coarse. There is a great difference between the fine feelings generated in a person by say a beautiful sunset, a fine picture or a sonnet by Shakespeare or the much coarser results engendered by unsavoury jokes or salacious gossip, as an example. The author would argue that the feelings induced by these very disparate experiences relate directly to the quality of the energies (unseen forces) the person is connecting too. The aggregate of experience eventually leads to the building of a person's character which is either fine or coarse (probably mostly a mixture unless that person is very self-determined), dependent upon what they have connected to in their life as a preponderance.

To continue the argument that there is far more to life than mere physical (and modern science itself confirms that how we see the world is entirely down to how our perceptions are "wired" -if you look at life through an electron microscope it appears quite different and a nuclear physicist would argue that this is the valid perception). So, pursuing this argument, one can certainly make the case that it is entirely possible that the ability to see auras, to be divinatory and even to recall clearly previous lifetimes is there, in actuality, at birth. Regrettably this is quickly overwhelmed by the over-powering cascade of planetary experience (although there is a great deal of evidence that suggests many children retain a memory of previous lives until they are at least three) and few youngsters live in a culture that encourages divinatory ability.

Beyond this (and this is particularly pertinent to the contents of this book) there are some who have had out- of-body experiences, particularly as a result of the shock of an accident as an example. For some this constitutes an epiphany, as it offers incontrovertible

THE LIVING EVENT OF THE HUMAN LIFE

evidence that they are not their physical body but an occupant of it; unless the familiarity of day-to-day life suppresses it, this kind of event can irrevocably change a life and set the person's feet on a new path of discovery. If we liken the body to the car we drive, after years of loyal service it may have to go to the scrap-yard, but that doesn't mean the occupant of the car has to go with it!

The purpose of this book is to explore the human event and its origins in far greater depth than previous knowledge has made possible. The reader needs to start with the notion that Life itself is far more than the physical world we see around us, that what we see is, for the most part, governed by the limitations of the body and its current settings – in the same way that a radio tuned to only Radio 3 will only pick up Radio 3, even though it has the potential to pick up hundreds of different signals if it is reset to its original design intent.

In addition to this, scientists have now found evidence that the Brain itself practices what is called "synaptic pruning", which means that it vigorously cuts away connections that a person doesn't use. At the same time oligodendrocytes in the brain are attracted to the pathways or axons we use the most and start to build a white myelin sheath (white matter) around them which increases the speed of transmission of the information, creating super highways in the brain and perfecting our usage of it. This means that eventually each person's brain is unique by usage (if not by original design) but it also means that much of the greater human possibility has been reduced by non-usage or by focusing on activity that is not beneficial to the individual life (clearly, there is some repetitional usage such as being depressed or developing a negative self-view that everyone can do without!). Obviously, a person who suffers lack of confidence needs to try to avoid the processes that promote lack of confidence,

PREFACE

which is harder to do once those pathways are engraved neurally. Where developing natural human abilities is concerned, the old adage "use it or lose it" is truly and frighteningly apt. However, not to be too down-hearted, because the right order of work can most certainly lead to the re-establishment of lost connections.

Furthermore, it is also important for the reader to understand that this work starts with the premise that Creation and the Planet we live on have practical purposes of their own and that any human endeavour that is real and actual must clearly comply with the intentions of the place in which they find themselves domiciled – just as, if you want to follow a career in a large business enterprise you are expected to comply with the aims, intentions, standards and protocols of the company. No company is going to tolerate an employee who is an unruly brigand who does not comply with its aims and intentions for very long.

At the moment, humans find themselves appearing at the end of our planet's history, a very long way from the origins of a Creation that is still expanding and growing. Here, on this Planet, there is currently a great deal of licence alongside a fantastic opportunity. In some ways, the Planet today may be regarded as a "nursery" for life form and we all know that, in a nursery there is a degree of flexibility and licence for behaviour because it is understood that the inhabitants are young and still "learning the ropes". Twenty years later, the young person is deemed to have reached the age of responsibility and much more is expected of them. In a way, the human, despite its cleverness and technological prowess, is a child in the face of Creation's magnitude and at some point, in its development journey, it will need to grow up.

If a person intends to pursue a career in a large business, it is

THE LIVING EVENT OF THE HUMAN LIFE

clearly their responsibility to become very well acquainted with the ways in which the business works, otherwise they will be of limited use in it. Equally, to fulfil a planetary and later creational purpose one must begin to build a deep understanding of the planetary and creational laws on which everything is based.

Everyone accepts that in order to grow properly, a plant, human or young animal needs the right conditions for life, and it is the same for the unseen parts of ourselves – once we have set our feet upon the development path, without the right conditions and opportunities we never reach our true potential in this particular life and can grow up stunted and unfulfilled. Admittedly, the founding premise of this book is that one can hopefully make a new approach in a future physical life, but then one will have an unfortunate personal history to undo.

It would be useful for the reader to begin with the notion that everyone has a genuine self, that is really them, together with a host of different roles that they are forced to adopt in order to survive in our culture. Everyone unconsciously understands this; we all realise that the person we share with our friends and family is probably not the person who we take to the office where the protocols of behaviour are probably quite different. In a way we are all actors and actresses par excellence and mostly people play their parts very well, even to the point where they confuse the role with their genuine self. Indeed, it is often when the person retires and finishes with the world of work that they feel bereft for they no longer have a theatre to play in – the role is no longer necessary and they feel lost without it because the real self is by now deeply buried.

A good beginning is therefore to realise that culture demands roles and a person needs roles to survive and make their way in the cultural collective. The genuine self also needs an arena in which to grow and develop and this is the world of Nature and Creation. It is for this reason that this work strongly features the need to study natural laws because these are the media through which the Planet and Creation speak to us.

Fortunately, even today the Planet still is a living embodiment of the natural laws and ways a person needs to build their life upon; it just takes time and the right kind of work, although it is much easier to do it with the right kind of help and companions. Furthermore, these laws are essentially simple and the study of them is not difficult or onerous but joyous and uplifting because they are the way we ourselves work. They give a person a framework on which to build the genuine self and give a deep understanding of the reasons for things that helps a person not just with their real life but even with their life within the culture. Working against natural law can only bring failure, stress and difficulty; working with nature reaps incredible success – if you have any doubt about this, talk to a gardener!

Note beforehand; this book is accompanied by the Afterlife Chart which can be found at the back and which should help the reader navigate successfully through the various chapters. There is also a Glossary of definitions of words used within the Book that are most likely unfamiliar to the reader and can be used as a quick reference.

Chapter 1: Number 1
From Pre-life to Pregnancy
Stage 1

The origins of Creational Structure; the need for Life to live, serve and maintain it; Creational Law and the significance of the Law of Three; the beginning of life (the Spawning); the Entity of Self; the actuality of life at planetary level. The situation prior to actual conception: the gathering of Alive; the winning edge of impossibility (the enormous odds against a successful physical appearance); Cultural influence (the situation now); the Natural Laws (the fatality of Life at Planetary level).

CREATION OF LIFE

NUMBER 1

The Making: In which the original entity of self forms up.

The first thing a person needs to grasp when approaching this vast and important subject is that, with respect to Creation and the origins of life this is unknown territory for the vast majority of people and even science is only just beginning to make tentative assays into it. So best to put all pre-conceived notions and ideas on one side and try to appreciate that the understandings and views expressed in this book are entirely new and not to be found anywhere in recorded history nor within the annals of religion or science.

Before we even begin to think about physical life on the planet or even the afterlife it is vital to consider what the situation might have been prior to existence here, in that for everything and everyone there had to be a first life. This is very important because it constitutes our origins, so to begin, we will look at the situation in Creation prior to the inception of Life. (It is appreciated that this can only be an academic premise at the moment but it is important to set the scene).

In the first place, Creation, in partnership with the Universe, created Structure. which, for the purposes of clarity, can be likened to the physical framework of a house. You have to start with the house – rather than the living occupants – and this is really a good analogy because houses need to be maintained. Without steady maintenance things wear out and in the same way Creation, in time, itself suffers entropy which stands against the urge to grow and evolve. It was for this reason that Creation had to agree to sponsor LIFE, in that there was clearly a need to SERVICE and MAINTAIN the STRUCTURE. It is for this reason that LIFE exists and has permission to LIVE, SERVE or MAINTAIN. These are the only options available to it; life can simply LIVE, and by living and processing the right energies give back to the place in which it lives. Or it can opt to serve, which means to take on some form of duty or it can aim at being part of the maintenance system, which really offers the greatest freedom of all because, after all, maintenance teams have to go everywhere!

It is interesting to note in passing that in the ancient Brahmananda Purana[1] it states that at first there was nothing but an eternal ocean, out of which a golden egg called Hiranyagarbha emerged and Brahma created himself within it. First, he made creation, the earth and other things, later he made people to populate his creation. So, first of all there was a containment (the egg) after which came the structure (the earth) and finally there was life.

An important consideration in all this is that many ancient myths concerning the origins of creation start with the idea of endless waters – all Egyptian myths begin with this concept and from this arises the Benben stone, which is a pyramid form (the prototype of the capstone for all pyramids to come). As John West remarks in "The Serpent in the Sky", the creation of the universe is a mystery" but "in Egypt this was regarded as the only ineluctable mystery"[2]. The Egyptians called it "the Primordial Scission" and considered that "Everything else is in principle comprehensible." (Page 33)

---

[1] The Brahmanda Purana is a Sanskrit text and one of the eighteen major Puranas, a genre of Hindu texts.

[2] John Anthony West, Serpent in the Sky, May 1993, Quest Books, US, ISBN 978-0835606912

NUMBER 1

It is fascinating that for the Egyptians the first manifestation from the primeval waters is the pyramid form of the Benben (which has four triangular faces), because the most important feature of all this is the fact that **all Creational Law** works on the TRIANGLE, the Law of Three, as exemplified by Positive, Negative and Neutral (and a host of others). Indeed, the triangle is the strongest structure there is. We can see many examples of this, and of special significance is Carbon, Oxygen and Nitrogen which constitute the building blocks of creation. The significance of three is further enshrined in religion and mythology, although perhaps few people are aware of the deeper meaning of it - one only has to think of the Christian trinity, the Hindu Brahma, Vishnu and Shiva, or the three Norse Norns to give but a few examples. It is, therefore, hardly surprising to find that Life requires three ingredients to function no matter where it appears in Creation. At the CORE of every living thing there have to be three ingredients that are issued at the point of Creational Spawning which is the point at which the origins of existence came together. This happened after the development of structure and was the initiation of life itself (but since then there have doubtless been many spawnings to facilitate creational need and this is explored later in this chapter.)

LIFE gives ALIVE to the affair but in order to form this vital trilogy, Being and Elemental (explained in more detail later) are also necessary.

BenBen Stone from the Pyramid of Aenehmat III

17

THE LIVING EVENT OF THE HUMAN LIFE

Originally, Creation donated some of its BEING but there are two kinds of BEING, the first given by Creation itself, the second known as LOCAL BEING. This washed down Creation to local constellations, solar systems and stars. So, for us, living on Planet Earth, the likelihood is that our source of BEING (which is an important part of the original Entity of Self) is the local constellations rather than the originating point of Being in Creation.

Everything needs a physical space, shape and form in which to occur, and virtually everything in Creation requires organic life, even though that may be far more rarefied (less dense) than our own. The final ingredient of the CORE has to be specific to locality, so here we must refer to Planet Earth, which like all planets is hungry for life form. The Planet has a great deal of ELEMENTAL being, given that her origins are ELEMENTAL. Indeed, it was powerful cone-shaped elemental forces which helped form and maintain the planet in the first place and elementals are still a vital part of her maintenance today.

So, the Planet puts ELEMENTAL into the pot, but in doing so the new CORE, issued from the Spawning and carrying a Creational and Constellational pedigree, has to agree to local protocols and criteria (the Laws at planetary level). This constitutes a CREATIONAL BYPASS as the Creational Content has to stand in **OBEYANCE** to the local point of appearance. (This simply means that everything on the Planet has to obey the local laws in the same way as the human body is designed to eat certain kinds of food and if you try to give it deadly nightshade, as an example, there are disastrous consequences). It is also worth remarking here that no life can exist here on the Planet unless it is contained in a physical form.

Consequently, all LIFE here on the Planet carries Creational Content but it is subdued by local conditions simply because for the higher echelons of Creation to appear here would be catastrophic for the Planet, in the same way as if someone were able to bring a teaspoon of Sun level here it would have dire consequences for us.

It is interesting to note that before conception, the pre-life form probably has a simple knowing of self; in a way, there is a first conception prior to the physical making, when the Being and the Elemental are conceived in the Creational Alive. These three constitute **an Entity**. At this point, Life itself claims the You – this is your point of origin and gives you a very high pedigree though you are not an individual at this point, that comes later, after you have developed the right kind of identity.

Nonetheless, right from the start, the Planet places limitations upon our Creational Content because she has her own purposes for organic life to fulfil; subsequently, the culture we find ourselves born into has its own agenda and this immediately reduces our possibility, so right from the start human life here is twice removed from its divinity and pedigree, once by the Planet and then by the culture in which we are born.

So, it is important to understand that for each planetary life form we see, something existed before its conception here on this planet. The planet is a living part of the great web of Creation and has to work in concordance with creational and natural law, just as a liver cell inside the human body has to work within the laws that govern that body. Although the idea of laws governing the planet may seem obscure and academic, they are actually very simple and obvious; if you turn on the tap you always get water, not coca-cola, if you throw a stone up in the air it comes down – and Life would

THE LIVING EVENT OF THE HUMAN LIFE

be a nightmare if this were not the case because all here relies on the dependability of the laws. Farmers and gardeners throughout the world base their entire lives on the continuance of the seasons, and these are governed by the Planet's relationship with the Sun. Moreover, in the same way that a living cell is composed of a central nucleus and in the cytoplasm, organelles, the Solar system in which we live is the equivalent of a single cell in the make-up of Creation. It is made up of the Sun, which is the nucleus and the surrounding planets (the organelles) each of which have a specific function within the solar system.

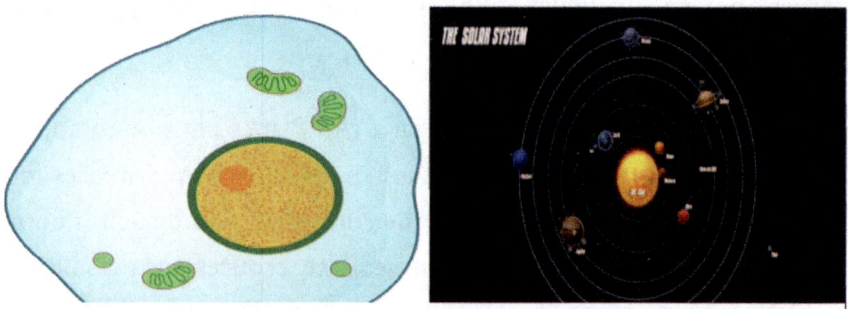

A side-by-side representation of a single cell and the Solar system

It is appreciated that this is new and complex knowledge so, to reiterate, we live within a system that is governed by the law of three. Creational law – like sunlight which is composed of the visible light spectrum, ultra-violet and infra-red – is triadic in nature so, as one would expect, and there are three core ingredients of the entity which exists before conception. It is very important to grasp this because those three ingredients – the Alive, the Being and the Elemental - constitute the raw ingredients of the original entity.

The planet exists as part of the solar system and needs life forms

NUMBER 1

to fulfil and support her purpose, to act as aerials for the signals she needs to harvest from Creation, as surely as we need to gather oxygen from the atmosphere to live. Just as a mobile phone or a TV aerial receives signals in order to function, a human being constantly takes in signals from its planetary surroundings and beyond.

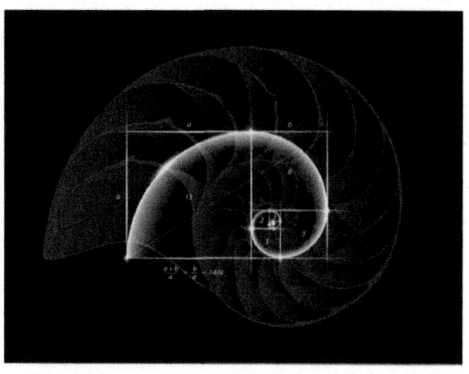

The Fibonacci Sequence a natural numbering system used by ancient Egyptians to build their temples; also seen extensively in India.

Everyone understands that in order to live virtually all life forms need physical food, water and air, but what is less understood is that all life requires electrical signals of the correct denomination to continue. Everything a life form takes into itself through its senses constitutes an electrical impression, and each impression is on a gradient from fine to coarse. The finer the signal the finer the life form; the more coarse the signal, the less refined the life form.

As the planet is part of the solar system which in turn is part of the Galaxy and Creation, each species of life here requires input from the planet (in the form of Elemental), input from the Sun, Solar system or local constellations (known as local Being) and crucially, the Creational Alive (which could also be described as "animating spirit"). It is the view of the writers of this book that without these three ingredients, which constitute a functioning CORE, nothing living could occur here on the planet, it would simply be minerals and rocks.

THE SPAWNING

The Origins of Life in Creation

In order to understand these key concepts, a person needs to realise that all levels of Creation have some form of life and that that life will have its own biology. It is folly to imagine that this tiny planet is the only place in Creation that supports life, though clearly the form that life takes may be very different to life here in that it will conform to different planetary laws and functions.

To further understand the key concept of Creational spawning (which is the means by which creation populates the various levels of itself), a person needs to study spawning as it occurs on planet Earth. This is a fascinating example of the ancient understanding "as above so below", essentially a modern paraphrase of the second verse of the Emerald Tablets of Hermes Trismegestes. Essentially this says that everything that occurs on the planet has its parallel in creation itself and the coral spawning is a marvellous example of this, even down to the fact that like the ocean, Creation itself experiences tides that periodically wash through it.

Every year, multiple species of coral spawn over several days following the Full Moon in September and October. Synchronising their response to the same signal, the coral releases millions of seeds into the oceans of earth where they are carried hither and thither by the ocean tides taking their chances in a great free-for- all. Another perhaps more easily accessible example is that of fungi, which also release millions of spores to be spread on the wind, often many miles across country.

NUMBER 1

The coral of Creation is in truth the Constellations and at times Life rattles the constellations and Spawning occurs; just as the coral spawn drifts through the oceans of earth so the Creational Alive issues from the constellations seeking FORM that will give it shape and even some physicality in which it is contained.

Brain coral spawning and dandelion seeds taking flight

Coral and fungal spores have a physical containment and can easily be seen. Equally, the Creational "Alive" is composed of minute balls of energy, sometimes known as "Orbs" that travel in our Solar system blown along by the Solar wind. Just as it is possible to see the spores of coral and fungi, it is possible for the sensitive and open-minded person to spot these tiny balls of energy.

An example of Orbs which can often be seen in nature as long as you take the time to look.

The creational spawning process is as arbitrary as that which determines the fate of the coral spawn; it may end up on a star, on another planet billions of light years away from here, it may end up in the constellations or it may bypass the higher echelons of Creation and end up here, on Planet Earth. It may never find a form and shape in which to lodge itself and as a consequence withers away. Wherever it ends up, the Creational Alive is key to the maintenance of life throughout Creation and is totally committed to the struggle of Creation to grow and evolve. It perhaps also accounts for the sense in higher life forms that they need to refine and reach for something higher to "go home" in the same way that the salmon are instinctively driven to return to the source of their arising.

Just like the coral spawn, where the creational spawn ends up is random; it could have been diverted into a cluster or a constellation, but that which ends up in life at planetary level has drifted a long way from its origins. It is also interesting to note that in the beginning, the Planet was hungry for the Creational Alive because she herself was at the start of her evolutionary journey. Now, the Planet is overloaded with life force and because of the unique circumstances at play here (the result of a long and often regrettable history) there is an abundance of people looking to reincarnate (hence the population explosion) so what powers new life form is likely to be indigenous to this Planet rather than new issue (known hereafter as "newbies") from Creation itself. Nonetheless, it is important to remember that even if one's life today is a result of many reincarnations, everyone began as a "newbie" as a consequence of that Creational Spawning.

Further important considerations of the Spawning can only be here described as **"esoteric biology"**. This has to do with what is loosely called the chemistry between people and different domains and essentially it has to do with attractions between things. Clearly, there are aspects of life that are drawn together; there are things that have an affinity between each other and things that are repelled by each other. This is an essential expression of the law of opposites (known also as the Law of Two) which everything on the planet is subject to. For those who live at the outer limits of Creation, this presents as a mystery; we do not understand, as an example, what drives attraction between things – what as an example, drives the sperm to the ovum (or is it the ovum that attracts the sperm?) What we experience is a vast collective web in which being of kind and wanting to be with others like us is very important. It is also obvious if one considers how most species want to be with others of kind, the old truism "birds of a feather flock together "is certainly very apt here. This has to do with having the right inner CONTENT, because it is this that is going to eventually support and nourish the **Entity of Self**.

It is also very interesting to consider, when exploring the "biology of Creation", the movement at planetary level from **Chaos to Criteria**. Clearly, if a person traces the development of different species on earth there is clearly a refinement process at play; there is after all, a great difference between the clunky appearance of a dinosaur and the delicacy of a butterfly or even the innate range and versatility of a species like ourselves. There have undoubtedly been moments of great change in the planetary story including leaps between species (astonishing and dizzying as the jump between synapses that occur between neurons in the brain – this is clearly a facsimile for how evolution happens). There has also been great differentiation between the species of life here - scientists tell us that life began in the sea, in water, and moved from there to land (earth) and today the Planet supports life like birds that are able to move between the elements of earth, air and even water. This is the

THE LIVING EVENT OF THE HUMAN LIFE

Planet exploring her own possibility and range and creating different options for her own evolution. It also reflects back into Creation, for this is clearly what Creation itself is doing.

In considering **Rhythms and Ascent** (remember we are still examining the Spawning) the Planet herself clearly has an incipient urge to refine, grow and ascend the creational bar. Ascent happens when things are joined or added to by domains that improve their possibility; this gives things the possibility of a greater EVENT OF LIFE. Again, this is not a random process but governed by creational cycles, exactly like the seasons we experience on earth.

This means that the human race, now living at the end of history and burdened with wrong manufacture that has taken it down an evolutionary cul-de-sac, still has an insipient urge to improve and grow.

The Spawning itself is a powerful explosion of speed, power and vibration and all these things have to have a rhythm which is compatible with each other and work in harmony, in the same way that the different speeds and rhythms of the different lives in the human body have to synchronise, otherwise it simply won't work. Imagine the chaos in a car engine if the gearing didn't synchronise.

The Planet herself is clearly following an **ascensional path**; the refinement and development of her expression (in the form of a multiplicity of different life forms) ultimately leading to an Elevation of process which will result in her becoming a star. (Barring accidents, even for the Planet nothing is guaranteed. She is gambling with her life as much as we with ours).

If we consider ascent from the point of view of the human species, this leads us to greater learning, greater awakening (in the sense of cognisance of our purpose here) and being more alive. However, it must be appreciated here that this relates to the emancipation of the real Entity of Self (as issued in the original coming-together on the planet) rather than the further development of wrong identity, which can only lead to ignorance, illusion and egotistical ideology, all of which are the heralds of descent. It is very important to understand that the Entity of Self is the real person that sits at the core of each one of us. We will keep coming back to this because it is the central tenet of this book.

It must be remembered that originally the Spawning was a Creational event but as Creation has gone on some of that event has been diverted away from its original purpose. Other purposes have crept in which were perhaps not planned for, just as when coral spawns on earth a multitude of other life forms turn up to feed. There is an ultimate purpose for the Spawning which has to do with the Entity of Self but because we live at the end of history other things have happened that have diverted things away from their original path. Firstly, the original spawning was diverted into the Solar system, meaning it bypassed the constellational level and turned up at a lesser level. This took it a step away from its **original Creational pedigree**.

Subsequently, it found itself on a planet which has had a long and unfortunate history and in which the human has **deviated from planetary purpose** and become something of a maverick. This further removes it from its original caste or pedigree. It is important to realise that this is not the human's fault but nonetheless in approaching the subject of human development and refinement it is important to understand the actuality of one's situation. This is rather like when you buy a house, the wise purchaser instructs a surveyor first so that one is forewarned about future problems and likely expenses.

To further reflect on this, it is clear that to grasp the proposition of being human and to start to build the original Entity of Self is going to involve a great deal of **struggle simply because none of us are actually WHAT we should be**. To continue the simple analogy of the house, probably none of us are "new builds", we all of us carry a history possibly way beyond this life. This is understandably hard for the reader to grasp initially even though they may intuitively sense it, but one only has to look at history and the current human condition to appreciate that life here is very far from being perfect. Furthermore, everything on the Planet has to be maintained – anyone who has ever owned a house or a car will appreciate this. Equally, SELF has to be maintained and it requires a great deal of **self-discipline** to do this. Always will high pressure chase low pressure and it is most important to maintain the real person in oneself; if the life has a powerful inner life (being) then it requires an equally powerful outward expression (elemental) otherwise the entire system grinds to a halt.

Moving on to the considerations of **Actuality and Conscious Ways**, it must be appreciated that the **original individuality** of the Entity of Self requires a **singular view in its CORE**. A person must realise that the bulk of Creation is **collective**, where everything thinks, feels and acts the same and the proposition of being a **unique individual** is rare. It has probably only come about here as a result of the difficult and unusual conditions of life here. Individuality (powered by the Creational Alive and sometimes Spirit) requires an identity that matches the real self and can be seen in the Works of Life that a person might build and surround themselves with. These are in no way **roles of life** which for the most part usurp the individuality of the person and fail to nourish their real life.

Further to this it is important to realise that for anything to come to this Planet it has to come through the Solar Cell itself, and in so doing it loses its identity or sense of self. This is why high forces from outside of solar, such as Spirit lose their identity and turn up as **fuel**. Furthermore, although the original spawning issued from the constellations, the solar system itself is now able to take over its function and is able to granulate and spawn itself.

Alongside the issue of Spawning, one needs to consider that Creation is vibrant, alive and always changing; things are drawn to other things by great **tidal influences** that wash between structures. Nothing is fixed. At certain times constellations, as an example, will be powered and at other times not, everything depends upon Creation's requirements for Maintenance and Life. The Spawn is drawn by different tides to different places by Creational need. It is appreciated that this is difficult to grasp and none of this will surrender to cultural thinking processes; probably the best way to get some sense of it is to **visualise** it as the way of it needs to come via the higher processes of the human mind — spending time watching the tide coming in, developing sensitivity to the passage of the seasons on earth, even sensing one's own breathing or feeling one's own heart beat will tune a person in to the great patterns and cycles of life which surround us.

THE LIVING EVENT OF THE HUMAN LIFE

PRE-CONCEPTION

The Gathering of Alive

Creational tides bring the fine CONTENT of ALIVE to the Planet from the Constellations and even the Solar System itself, which has a huge demand for life form to serve its purposes. Everything on the planet – from a butterfly to an ant to a human- grasps something of the Creational Alive before its initial conception; it cannot be formed or function without it. The Creational Spawn, in its turn, is also hungry for life shape and form for if it doesn't find a suitable host, it withers as surely as the coral spawn that fails to find the right environment in which to survive. It must be pointed out that there is nothing religious in this; there is no pre-destination, it is as arbitrary as a roulette wheel. The Alive that powers an ant is identical to the Alive that powers a human being; there is a mutual need in the life form and the Alive entity which is satisfied when the two come together.

Obviously, if we survey the multiple life forms which proliferate on the planet, we see that what the human can do by pedigree and assembly, that is the human's long history of acquired experience and refinement of stock - is far greater than say, an ant or a buffalo. The human is the optimum life form here and has the greatest possibility, even if its acts and the outplay of its life falls far short of its possibility. It is also vital to grasp that the original triadic appearance – the Elemental, the Being and the Creational Alive – constitute a unique core which is seeking expression (through form and shape), emancipation and fulfilment of self at the level it finds itself. Obviously, once the Creational Alive is committed to a particular life form the decision is final and irrevocable; the laws of

Creation do not work with erasers to hand!

Clearly, the Core of all LIFE here is looking for a winning edge in the face of impossible odds not only because of the roulette wheel of where it appears — with limited options if it finds itself in say, an ant — but also because even if it finds itself lucky enough to turn up in human form it then faces a future in a world that is very far from ideal or how Creation would have it be.

THE WINNING EDGE OF IMPOSSIBILITY

(The enormous odds against a successful physical appearance...)

Perhaps this is the moment for a person to reflect on the extraordinary odds against turning up not only on a Planet that was hungry for life in the first place (rather than drifting on into oblivion), but also turning up in the form of the most advanced species on the face of the Earth, rather than in the form of an ant or a rhinoceros as an example. The odds are billions to one against waking up inside the human possibility, especially if one factors in the millions of sperm racing to fertilise one egg. The odds against any one of us actually being born are staggering especially when one considers that nothing anywhere is **GUARANTEED**. Certainly, if a person truly grasps the extraordinary odds that they have overcome just to be here, it should cause awe and a great urgency in themselves to make the most of the incredible opportunity that living represents.

CULTURAL INFLUENCES

(The situation now...)

A further consideration of the pre-life settings (that is before anything enters a physical body) has to be the fact that, in turning up on this Planet the new issue is turning up in a **ready-made culture** that is far removed from the natural culture that would have originally existed here and which would have been tailor-made for the **Planet's purposes**.

Culture arises wherever there is more than one person. Cultures are born from similarities of purpose, sympathy in the sense of mutual connections within a living event or collective and synchronisation at the hands of those in charge who exert control and privilege and who govern the indoctrination of the people. Whatever culture a person is born into, one falls within its jurisdiction and control in so far as it is the culture that determines the arena in which a person can operate; what would be available to say, an Aztec child two thousand years ago would have been very different to what is available today for a child born into a modern culture. Therefore, the culture has a bearing upon the pre-conceptual event of life which cannot be dismissed.

THE LIVING EVENT OF THE HUMAN LIFE

THE NATURAL LAWS

(The fatality of life at planetary level...)

Finally, in considering the making of the **Entity of Self**, one cannot ignore the **Natural Laws** which are the determining factor in what happens here and what happens to the entity prior to physical conception. All laws are catalytic to what happens around them and they represent criteria to which all are subject – otherwise a human mother could give birth to anything. Fortunately, the laws ensure that she gives birth to something human. One's beginning and one's making are all subject to **Natural or Organic Law** which specifies that nothing can happen unless there are three influences acting on the same spot at the same time. Whenever a person sees an example of the Law of Two (sometimes referred to as **opposites** such as birth/death, hot/cold etc) they are actually seeing the **Law of Three** and it is that third aspect, sometimes difficult to spot, that makes things occur. In the scenario of life origin, the Being, the Elemental and the Creational Alive constitute the Entity of Self. At the point of physical conception, the mother's ovum, the father's sperm and the Entity itself come together and the eventual containment of the life starts to form up. In this way, a person's beginning and making are all subject to natural laws and the very same laws that Creation itself operates on.

NUMBER 1

Here are some examples to get you started; can you think of any more?

Positive	**Negative**	**Neutral**
Height	Depth	Breadth
Caterpillar	Chrysalis	Butterfly
Man	Woman	Child
Sun	Moon	Planet
Youth	Adulthood	Old Age
Convex	Concave	Flat

Chapter 2:
Pre Life Settings

A further exploration of the situation prior to the first physical life; the impact of time, human origins, Antiquity and the modern world; locating oneself on the Planet; the Entity of Self or individuality versus the collective; The considerations of Place and Form (in which we explore the Actuality of Life Upon the Planet); the considerations of the "as What": the True Entity of Self offset to the Human Historical Inheritance; Something else (Lack of Perfection impacting on the Design); the Collective (the Altogether as a Single Entity and Mind).

THE LIVING EVENT OF THE HUMAN LIFE

In this chapter, the reader is introduced to an in-depth appreciation of the overwhelming series of events that occur prior to the unborn child's appearance in the world.

Today, because the modern human is largely only aware of their physical circumstance, they lack something of a natural cognisance of the **AVALANCHE** of unseen influences that bombard the unborn within the womb. These influences (both natural and unnatural) constitute a vast web of **PRE-PHYSICAL LIFE** Settings which the mother is mostly oblivious of but are nonetheless very real and constitute a potent marinade for all that is still unborn.

In the first place, the growing embryo finds itself locked in a planetary environment and subject to **Time** in a way that is entirely new to it. It has a species and planetary timetable beginning at conception alongside everything else that lives and is organic. The reader must understand that different species and different epochs run at different times – a shrew, as an example, only lives for a year, but it ages at the same rate as us and there is every reason to think that for the shrew its time is equivalent to our seventy or eighty years. In John Downer's "Supersense: Perception in the Animal World"[1] he notes that "anyone who has tried to swat a fly will know that its reactions are almost instantaneous. Its eyes can discern very small intervals of time (it can respond to a falling hand in less than one hundredth of a second) and our clumsy attempts to kill it must appear ponderously slow, as if filmed in slow motion". Equally, "the cockroach has a similar high- speed existence and can react to any

---

[1] John Downer *Supersense: Perception in the Animal World* page 141, BBC Books November 1988 (ISBN 0-563-20660-8) supported with a six-part documentary series

attempt to crush it in s fiftieth of a second, while our own reaction time is a tenth of a second."

It is very clear that time and speed are very species specific. Equally, the time needed to create a suitable body for the species and to integrate that life form into the body (a new machine) varies enormously from specie to specie. At the same time, one must appreciate that Cultures move at different speeds – our culture is super-fast, things are changing today at phenomenal rates whereas when reflecting back on history we can see that the way of life and people's experience stayed the same for millennia. Human life was governed by the spiral of seasons, the rhythm of day and night rather than the movement of hands on the clock. (Although, time-keeping devices go back many thousands of years, modern pendulum style clocks were originally invented by European medieval monks who wanted to regulate their lives to conform to their Church discipline). Once every church tower or town hall had a clock, living became regulated by that rather than the natural rhythms of life. By the time of the Industrial Revolution, people were already forced to regulate their lives according to the clock because industry and technology demanded it. The factory system demanded that people came to work at a specific time and left at a specific time and even meal times and toilet breaks were strictly regulated.

These are some of the reasons why humans today would look at things very differently from people from Antiquity and it is really quite impossible to understand ancient cultures, such as Egypt, Sumeria or Assyria through the prism of modern thinking. It is like looking at a different species. To understand these something like Ancient Egypt, a person has to put aside their personal prejudices and think like an Egyptian (very hard to do!)

PRE LIFE SETTINGS

It is clear that for Creation itself, Time happens very differently, and the experience of Time alters as Life in Creation steps down through different levels. Our experience of time is very subjective, even if it feels real to us; in truth, actual time is only possible at an actual Creational Event. It must be considered here because the pre-life human form is about to enter a world where Time is measured obsessively and in which their own species has an allotted term of life. (An interesting aside, however, is, in examining the credible stories of people who have reincarnated their experience between lives does not seem to relate at all to the planetary passage of physical time).

So, although Time doesn't struggle it is the cause of a struggle in life itself, which has deadlines to reach, in the sense that each species has an allotted time span in which to reach its optimum-just as the produce of the Spawning has a circumscribed time in which to find a suitable life form. Alongside that, the Planet has her own purposes – inextricably linked to her own evolutionary path – and from the start all new life is closely bonded to that planetary purpose even though life itself may have a creational origin and intent beyond that. Furthermore, the growing embryo is linked through the mother to a transient (family) line originating as far back as the beginning of Antiquity; thus, the influence of history, forefathers and especially the planet herself have sway over all organically developing life forms.

Unfortunately, the negative impact of history and antiquity has already insinuated itself into the mother via the transient tree and may well have negative consequences on the yet to be conceived pre life form. The reader needs to appreciate that THE TRANSIENT LINE is the family tree that stretches back to the very origins of human life via the genetic line of the mother; this obviously carries strengths and limitations which are inevitably passed on through the mother (for a deeper appreciation of this see further work later in the book.)

Alongside all of this, every specie is limited by the constraints of WHAT it is for and WHAT it is not and these represent a PARADIGM outside of which nothing can exist without further evolutionary input. So, the more the new arrival travels into the planetary domain the more it experiences constraints on its freedom.

Since the beginnings of history, there have been thousands of diverse cultures that have followed each other in an unbroken line through the various epochs, culminating in the present. The influence of these cultures can still be felt today as their accumulated knowledge and physical alteration of natural connection and practice has enabled and contributed to the making of life as it is today. In addition, the Planet is contained within the Van Allen Belts and all the signals ever issued here are recorded forever in what is commonly known as the astral light and the akashic records. It is this that allows genuine "mumming" or passion plays to occur, always assuming that there are people available to divine and accurately portray the signal.

At the same time, there is an abundance of evidence that indicates that the Planet and its association with human life is far older than is generally thought. Not only does the technology of civilisations such as Ancient Egypt clearly date from far older periods than Egyptologists are prepared to acknowledge, there is a wealth of evidence that there have been very advanced cultures on the planet further back in antiquity than any modern scientist is willing to admit to. In Cremo and Thompson's book "The Hidden History of the Human Race" [2] (the condensed edition of Forbidden Archaeology), cite evidence such as "a metallic vase made of pure silver and blown out of Pre Cambrian rock 600 million years old in Dorchester Massachusetts in 1852", "a block wall of smooth polished stone found in an Oklahoma mine in 1928 in carboniferous coal that was probably 286 million years old" and "a metallic sphere from South Africa with three parallel grooves around its equator found in a Pre-Cambrian mineral deposit said to be 2.8 billion years old", to name but a few.

Evidence like this really makes a nonsense of the notion that anatomically modern human beings have only existed for the past two hundred thousand years and that human culture only began to work bronze and metal some three thousand years ago.

The Dorchester Vase

The research of authors such as Graham Hancock (Author of "Fingerprints of the Gods" and other books which challenge orthodox archaeology) and others clearly indicates that the real story of the human race is very different to the paradigm that conventional archaeologists and historians would have us believe.

In addition, with reference to the **Antiquity of Ancient Egypt,** the famous Greek historian Herodotus (fifth century BC) mentions

---

[2] Forbidden Archeology: The Hidden History of the Human Race Michael A. Cremo and Richard L. Thompson 1993 ISBN 978-0892132942 ISKCON Krishna

traditions of an immense pre-historic period of Egyptian civilisation in his History Book 2; in this, he mentions, without further speculation, information obtained from Egyptian priests at Heliopolis regarding their history which stated that "during this time there were four occasions when the sun rose out of his wonted place- twice rising where he now sets and twice setting where he now rises." The French mathematician Schwaller de Lubicz[3] interprets this as having to do with the precession of the equinoxes and convincingly proves it to be a period of thirty- nine thousand years prior to Herodotus (for further details see Pages 406-408 "Fingerprints of the Gods "Graham Hancock.)[4] The esoteric archaeologist John Anthony West ponders the mystery of Egyptian civilisation which appears to have sprung into existence with no prior history of development and concludes that the answer is obvious "Egyptian civilisation was not a 'development', it was a legacy."[5] All of this should whet the appetite of the reader and encourage them to do their own research into the extraordinary history of the Planet and the human race life upon it.

Essentially, everything has an origin and an antiquity; even what we experience today has its roots in the past and something already there just as today's people are making tomorrow's event. Equally, what a person was yesterday influences what they will be tomorrow

---

[3] René Adolphe Schwaller de Lubicz (December 30, 1887 – December 7, 1961) Sacred Science page 87 Sacred Science: The King of Pharaonic Theocracy (New York: Inner Traditions International, 1982) ISBN 0-89281-007-6

[4] Graham Hancock 2 August 1950 Fingerprints of the Gods pages 406 – 408 1995 Crown Publishing Group ISBN978-0517887295

[5] John Anthony West (September 7, 1932 – February 6, 2018) Serpent in the Sky: The High Wisdom of Ancient Egypt, Quest Books, 1979; page 1

and this will govern their future; in the event of an afterlife being an actuality, it can only be equivalent to the life a person is building now. Perhaps the best counsel comes from Marcus Aurelius (AD121 – 180) who wrote "Get busy with Life's Purpose, toss aside empty hopes, get active in your own rescue."

However, not to diversify too much but to return to the main theme of this book, it is important to appreciate that, for the Human, the modern era has seen an unprecedented surge of new ideas, new inventions, new values resulting in an unnatural speeding-up of life which would be completely disorientating for any species. Essentially, the Old and the New will always struggle against each other; this is manifest in the way young adolescents fight with their parents and vice versa —and this extends even into the animal realms. An ironic example of this is encapsulated in the realm of Christianity and its ongoing arguments about the respective merits of the Old Testament as opposed to the New Testament, and vice versa.

Returning to the theme of the pre-life, it is important to consider not just the overwhelming outside influences impacting upon the unborn child, but also the internal technology of a human life which is forming up in the midst of all this.

An essential part of the human core is **ELEMENTAL** (remember the original entity of self was Elemental Being, Planetary Being and Alive). Clearly, **ELEMENTAL** is to do with the **DOING** of things, **BEING** is exactly that, **being**. These two CORE aspects of human life equate to an OUTER life (Elemental) and an INNER life (Being) and it is vital that both aspects of SELF are fully realised, otherwise the process of LIVING comes to a stop.

TO DO with respect to the human body represents an

THE LIVING EVENT OF THE HUMAN LIFE

enormous challenge because compared to any other planetary life form – say a cow or an ant or a dog – the human machine is incredibly complex. So, to be able to effectively handle such a machine is an enormous task of far-reaching proportions, especially in a world where distraction is the order of the day.

The reader needs to understand that the origins of the human race as it stands today is the direct consequence of catastrophic events that lie deep in history and antiquity and still impact on our lives today. It is out of the question to go into this in detail here, but it is important that the individual appreciates that the long-term consequences of world history is not the human's fault. However, whilst abnegating blame it is important to realise that a person has to play "the hand" they are dealt and while it is appreciated that we live in most challenging times every human has certain aspects of self that are incontrovertibly positive, to wit the extraordinary abilities latent in the human design and the fact that the Planet and Nature continually demonstrate the correct way to proceed according to natural law. This will be explored in more depth in the following section.

THE CONSIDERATIONS OF PLACE AND FORM

To continue with the **considerations of pre-life settings** it is important to return to the Actuality of the human situation NOW.

Clearly the place where all this is occurring is here, on the Planet, and if we are dealing with human life, a pentagrammic **FORM**. Put simply, the human shape is a five-pointed star (unlike most fauna on the Planet) and this is indicative of a higher than planetary origin and possibility. (Obviously, if it is a different planetary life form not all the PRE-LIFE SETTINGS will apply). There is a whole raft of meaning behind the symbol of the pentagram and a great deal that the reader needs to understand about how it functions (and how they themselves function) but for now suffice it to say that there is nothing dark or sinister about the symbol. It is entirely natural and indicative of the very high origins and pedigree of the human being.

According to the Law of Two (the fundamental law here upon the Planet, often seen or referred to as opposites and frequently referred to in esoteric literature and by many great minds from the past, writers such as Ralph Waldo Emerson[6]), everything either yaws or pitches. Yawing is a spinning motion which draws in new experience and actuality, much as the Planet spins, draws in and thereby gathers the necessary frequencies to move on in her evolutionary journey. At a much higher level, it may be seen that time and space yaw and life pitches within it but it is beyond the

---

[6] Ralph Waldo Emerson (May 25, 1803 – April 27, 1882)

scope of this particular book to explore this now.

In much the same way, within the womb, the growing life form reaches a point when electrically, it spins, and in doing so starts to draw into itself higher manifestations that are able to attend the **Human Event,** such as the Way itself (to be dealt with in more detail later) as well other higher planetary life forms (such as Elemental) which have an interest in the affair. This would be a powerful driving force and motivation in the new life as it moves forward in its journey. It might also gather to itself contents, other life or even actual living forms – as an example, there may be **DUTY LIVES** with important content who are wishing to return to complete a tour of service which may attach themselves to the developing life. (It is appreciated that for those readers who are new to this order of work, the idea of lives deliberately opting to return to a physical life to complete a duty may seem odd and far-fetched, but it must be considered alongside the fact that in actuality everything on the Planet that is natural is striving to fulfil a planetary purpose that sits within the greater purpose of the Solar system, which itself sits within the greater purpose of Creation itself. For those lives or entities that are natural this is the sole purpose of their existence.)

However, to continue our exploration of the human technology itself and what is actually happening as the foetus develops, it must be said that alongside yawing, one has to consider **pitching**, which is the positive going forward influence and input of any event.

Pitching draws in experience and ability which is endemic to the human form and possibility, including the superior aptitude of the human brain and head life (so clearly enhanced beyond the level of most other planetary forms of life). It must be remembered that although the life form occurring here is planetary based, the original event has its origins in the Creational Spawning and therefore carries a very high promise and represents a space for life to occur or happen in.

Of course, the discerning reader will also spot that in actuality living itself can be visualised as an ongoing replay of pitch and yaw, in that the young child gathers experience that hopefully allows them to successfully pitch into life in whatever domain they are hoping to engage in, and in the natural order of things this would be repeated throughout their lives.

Further considerations of Place and Form include the repetitional manner in which the mother's thoughts and processes influence the growing child and, in turn, the growing child influences the mother. Clearly, much of everyday life is habitual and subject to routine and will of course have an effect on the feelings of the mother and in turn on the growing human life. However, despite the powerful empathic relationship with the mother, the growing life will still be aware of a growing sense of its own self. Also, it has long been well-known that traumatic events occurring to the mother during pregnancy can impact on the growing embryo, even to the extent of causing birth marks. This suggests that at this point memory structures have already been installed and are impacting on the unborn child. Indeed, some mothers today try to capitalise on this by playing certain kinds of music or reading certain kinds of literature to the unborn child in an effort to influence the eventual character of the infant. Clearly, external events already carry significance and it is for this reason, in ancient times, that confinement meant the seclusion of the pregnant mother for the duration of the pregnancy away from influences that could potentially harm the unborn child.

THE LIVING EVENT OF THE HUMAN LIFE

It is also important not to forget that the mother herself will have abilities and proclivities – such as an aptitude for Languages or Maths or a leaning towards the Occult and Esoteric – that can also transfer to the unborn.

THE CONSIDERATIONS OF THE "AS WHAT"

First of all, it is important to acknowledge that what we are is a consequence of the way life was made; we wouldn't be us if things had been as they should be- the truth of the matter is we are not natural – unlike the bulk of Earth's flora and fauna. If we were as we should be, no one would need to make an esoteric journey (the Way) and we wouldn't be talking about recovering the Entity of Self, simply because we would already be exactly what we were designed to be. Almost inevitably we would be part of a Collective, not a "personality collective" but a collective based upon function and purpose. This is almost certainly the case elsewhere in Creation, in places where planets have not suffered the unfortunate history of this one.

The only reason we can talk about the "as what" is the fact that, in this time and place, there is a choice for us; we are undeveloped because nothing here has lived up to expectations. This is why there has been a long history of so-called "saviours" on the planet, whose sole function has been to try to get the human race back on track, though the evidence appears to show that no matter the purity and integrity of the originating source of these teachings they have eventually drifted far from their origins in their expression. The WHAT has been overtaken by the WHO just as occurs in the story of individual lives. In the First Life, the person is closest to the real themselves; the further they move from that first appearance the more they develop a "who" and the more they start to join with a collective, given that the moment there is more than one of something protocols of behaviour have to be established in order to peacefully co-exist. Hence, WHAT is the first life; WHO is subsequent lives, although obviously that who is going to be further from or closer to the embedded core, depending on the PERSON.

From the standpoint of the Planet and Creation, it is the **"what"** of the growing life form that is important rather than the **"who"**; Creation and the Planet are pragmatic and practical where life form is concerned, they are interested in WHAT SERVES THEIR PURPOSES.

Equally, if a person is interested in rediscovering and developing their real self, they too need to be addressing WHAT they are rather than who they are.

Looking at the developing life form, it constitutes an Entity appearing at planetary level with sun level input and with the ALIVE (creational issue) sitting in the CORE.

Alongside this, the Entity recognises the pedigree and antiquity of the mother carried by her transient line connections, along with eminent possibility installed in the growing child pre-birth. This requires lengthy explanation but suffice it to say, briefly here, that eminent connection stretches beyond the planetary and opens doorways to the **Ascensional Way**, should the new life be able to reach that far (Ascensional to mean the path beyond planetary leading to the upper echelons of Creation itself). This is obviously deep and profound work that needs to be explored in much more detail at a later date, but it is important that the discerning reader is aware of it as part of the human promise.

But, returning to the proposition of starting the journey of self in a physical body at planetary level it is important to note the following:

PRE LIFE SETTINGS

Alongside the influences of the mother and human history and at the same time, the Planet is asserting her own will and purpose via the developing machine (body) into which the ENTITY is growing. Even in the face of a human culture that manifestly fails to cleave to the natural order of things, the Planet tenaciously cleaves to her own purpose and origins, which is to develop and work in harmony with the purposes of the solar system and Creation itself. This is as mechanical as the purpose that drives the human body, in which each constituent part is unequivocally dedicated to the success of the whole machine. Unlike the human, neither the human body nor the Planet can choose not to serve its purpose (which is just as well really – neither the human body nor the Planet can be recalcitrant and decide not to give a hundred percent effort. The human body always does the best it can often in the face of considerable abuse from its occupant and the Planet never decides to take a day off and not spin or bother to produce air!)

Obviously, the new physical form is tailor-made for the purpose it was made to do – a dog to process dog force, an ant to process ant force, a human to process human and so on. These forces represent a multiplicity of different fuels and energies that the Planet herself needs to maintain herself and develop.

Part of the secret art of the mother is to successfully integrate the new entity into every cell of the new body thus allowing the new life the option to be fully itself once it is outside the mother and able to engage with the full promise of life.

Despite being bombarded with influences from outside the mother through her complex and persona, the new growing life will also experience a growing **awareness of self** within its inner life. Alongside this, the unborn life already experiences **pre-cognisant**

attachments to the unseen worlds that relate specifically to the manner in which the three component parts of the Entity of **Self**– namely, the Being (Planetary), the Elemental (Sun) and the Creational Alive – retain an empathic link with their point of origin. This washes through the mother and child during pregnancy and constitutes a cleansing and a reinforcement of the original purposes of the developing life form.

SOMETHING ELSE

There is something else to consider here. The point is, although Nature plans for a result, given that things are not perfect here, things do not always go to plan!

Firstly, the physical making of the new body may be inaccurate, in just the same way as you get "Monday morning" car manufacture! Secondly, if one considers the vast difference between the aptitude, the understanding, the mental ability of the majority of planetary life forms – whales, dogs, ants, cats etc – and that of the human being, it becomes clear that mankind has developed to a point far beyond the scope of planetary life. The difference is so enormous that a thinking person can only come to the conclusion that human possibility has been deliberately accelerated beyond planetary level and now finds itself accelerating well beyond the normal parameters of life here.

PRE LIFE SETTINGS

THE COLLECTIVE – THE ALTOGETHER AS A SINGLE ENTITY AND MIND

If one studies the vast majority of life forms on the planet it is clear that by and large, LIFE appears here as a COLLECTIVE, in which everything shares the same function and purpose and to understand one is to understand all. If one member of the COLLECTIVE learns something, everyone learns it.

This has been researched by the English biologist Rupert Sheldrake [7] who noticed that a useful change, discovery or understanding made by one entity in the animal kingdom was automatically transmitted to other groups (even overseas) within the same species. (He called this "morphic resonance" within and through fields of consciousness).

COLLECTIVE behaviour can easily be seen in the way groups of animals – packs of wolves, wildebeest, bees to name just a few– act as if they are ONE ENTITY rather than a group of individuals. All have the same mind set and purpose.

It is obvious that at planetary level (and possibly much of Creation), the COLLECTIVE and its guaranteed behaviour and process is of paramount importance as it guarantees a "return" to the planet and no argument with her purposes. One hardly expects a solitary bee to strike out independently and try to have an independent career of its own separate to the hive! Everything

---

[7] Alfred Rupert Sheldrake (born 28 June 1942)

THE LIVING EVENT OF THE HUMAN LIFE

within the COLLECTIVE thinks and acts the same, they have **a life of multiplicity and mind.**

On the other hand, the INDIVIDUAL, the so-called "free radical" that does not conform to the COLLECTIVE is dangerous (in that by behaving like a "wild card" it can deviate from the original purpose of the Planet or Creation and introduce toxic manufacture to the whole affair). But on the other hand, the free radical can be the media via which change and evolution can occur.

Human life form – unlike monkeys, apes or other simians- do not conform to a collective in that they do not act altogether as a SINGLE ENTITY and MIND. There are obvious exceptions to this in that there is crowd behaviour when humans respond to a collective impulse or, sinisterly, to a powerful individual or dogma bent on mass control. However, by and large, humans have the option to act individually or at least as part of a disparate group.

Clearly, at some point in human history, there has been a COLLECTIVE amnesty which has allowed INDIVIDUALITY to come forth (otherwise it would not be a possibility now) and the promise of this is carried forward into the growing life of the yet unborn baby. So, despite the collective influences washing over it, the new life is also cognisant of the bright flame of INDIVIDUALITY and UNIQUENESS burning within, the legacy of its Creational heritage. So, in this sense, the growing life awakens to a dualistic sense of "the single 'I' in relation to the collective 'I'".

As long as the person has to live alongside others, they become part of a Collective, whether that collective is being part of a family or part of a culture. So, from the start, there will be a struggle between the soon-to- be conceived life and the circumstances in which it finds itself appearing. This is likely to be replayed later in the physical life in that whatever situation the child finds itself in because it only has two choices – comply with the situation or be revolutionary to it.

THE CONSIDERATIONS OF THE TRANSIENCE

*Further considerations of the situation prior to **the first physical life**: Return of Kind; the 'newbie' and the significance of the transient line; time 'runners'; the Transcendental (greater promise of the human event); the possibility of greater self-connection.*

THE LIVING EVENT OF THE HUMAN LIFE

RETURN OF KIND

(The overwhelming natural urge to congregate with others of kind)

If a person looks at life on this planet, it is clear that the urge to be with kind, to return to kind is a dominant feature here. This can be easily seen in animal life, where wildebeest, zebras, polar bears and a host of other life forms choose to be together, even to the point of migrating and travelling together as a collective.

Clearly, all these species respond to a specific signal or set of signals and because animal life is natural, they respond to it in a pure way that carries through from generation to generation. This is perhaps most clearly seen in birds, about forty per cent of which migrate following the same signals for generation after generation and for thousands of years.

For humans, there is clearly a drive to mix with people with similar values, standards and backgrounds and a common point of reference is clearly family and the person's transient tree.

At this point in history, the situation where **"newbies"** (the first issue of Creational Spawning) is concerned is difficult because there is fierce competition for the opportunity to reincarnate from those who have come through previously. Amongst these, there may be members of the mother's transient tree linked by blood (which carries content and is itself highly occult) and family DNA who are looking for a new stab at life.

Consequently, the newbie can easily be "gazumped" by people looking for a Second life or even a new opportunity to reincarnate.

PRE LIFE SETTINGS

The **transient tree** of a person stretches far back into history and antiquity and, because the Planet herself is feminine, is headed up by Matriarchs (entities that live in the **ETHEREAL** realms of the planet herself).

Culturally, the purposes of the **TRANSIENT TREE** are something most people are unaware of but they are deeply engraved in the family lines themselves in a powerful unconscious fashion – you only have to look at the amount of emotion people invest in family and the sense of "belonging" to a group. Originally, the purposes of the transient tree would have been a guarantee to the Planet that certain attributes and qualities would be carried forward into the future to the point where she evolved into a star and required a finer life form. However, today it is unlikely that many people would be at all aware of the high origins and purpose of the matriarchs and most family lines are now entirely subverted into cultural preoccupations.

As a consequence of the human movement away from natural purpose, for the most part the new Creational issue from the Spawning is sacrificed on the altar of obedience to the transient line. It is certainly interesting how many people who claim to remember past lives believe themselves to be their own grandfather, grandmother or whatever. (It is recommended that readers who are interested in this take a look at Ian Stevenson, MDs excellent research "Children Who Remember Previous Lives".[8])

---

[8] Ian Pretyman Stevenson (October 31, 1918 – February 8, 2007) Children Who Remember Previous Lives: A Question of Reincarnation, Rev. Ed. (Revised) Paperback – 31 Mar. 2001 McFarland & Co 31 Mar. 2001 ISBN 978-0786409136

THE LIVING EVENT OF THE HUMAN LIFE

THE RUNNER

(Lives which are gearing up towards a fulfilment of purpose at a future date)

Alongside the transient line, there are others wishing to appear here who are in a sense "preborn" before the time they are best fitted to. They often have a deep inner knowing that they have a job to do in the future and they are in a sense "ticking over" until they reach a time which is the "best fit" for their actuality. These lives are also waiting to "hitch a lift" or "piggy-back" into their own future. This may also include duty and service lives who are looking for opportunities to fulfil an important planetary task here. Alongside the requirements of the family tree, small wonder there is such fierce competition for bodies here, especially in this time of great emergence and human potential.

TRANSCENDENTAL

(The greater promise of the human event)

Transcendental here means originating from a higher point of issue and has no spiritual connotations. In this context, "transcendental" is indicative of Sun or Solar possibility, whereas "transient" relates to the Planet herself. The fact that the human is pentagrammic is emblematic of its higher possibility which stretches beyond planetary and even beyond Solar, though it has to fulfil its Solar potential to accomplish this.

Furthermore, the prefix "trans" whether it refers to **transient, trans-solar** or **trans-celestial** is indicative of a journey that needs to be made from one state to another and the media via which the journey is accomplished. It must be remembered that everything on the planet is in a sense embryonic because the Planet herself is still developing. Transcendental signifies a generation and regeneration of content and suggests the Planet can "borrow" higher content that will help her evolve and develop beyond her present possibility.

Clearly, there is an ascending scale of domain bodies here on the Planet with a far greater range of ability and being able "to do" in the so-called higher life forms. (A human is able to do far more than say a dog, for a dog cannot write a play, paint a picture or develop far- ranging technology that shapes the very substance of the Planet herself.) Nevertheless, animal life is truer to its planetary purpose than its human counterpart because it is WHAT it should be, whereas the human has moved far away from its natural planetary origins.

The donkey, the cat, the rhinoceros are locked into planetary

THE LIVING EVENT OF THE HUMAN LIFE

purpose and their evolutionary possibility is inextricably linked to that of the Planet herself (unless they are able to "species leap" into human form). It is possible to change species and also gender at planetary level, but it does require the agreement and acquiescence of the Planetary CHROMOS to achieve this.

The Chromos is another vast realm of study but briefly it equates to the inner membrane that encloses a cell and governs what happens within the cell. Obviously, things within the cell have to maintain a certain balance, otherwise imbalance and ill-health happen as a consequence. In the same way, the Planetary Chromos governs what happens within the planetary domain and what is acceptable here. There is more flexibility on the Planet than there would be higher up Creation, but nonetheless everything at planetary level has to have a suitable container to exist in and to abide by the Laws here.

The signpost to superior possibility beyond the planetary domain is an enhanced mental possibility and the option to be CONSCIOUS rather than simply AWAKE to one's planetary situation.

The TRANSCENDENTAL is connected to the human promise of life and it is reiterated before a child is born by planetary agreement and the accord of higher planetary life forms, for example earth life elementals. If there were no such agreement the Human would simply not be able to live here.

GREATER SELF-CONNECTION - A COMMONALTY OF ASSOCIATION

(The option, unique to the human, to ascend above planetary)

Unlike other planetary life forms, the HUMAN is by pedigree, divinity and design pre-disposed to be able to "commute" to higher realms – initially Sun and Solar) – and to crystallise something of those realms in themselves and start to build embodiments from outside the planet. Part of the human promise of life is the option to ascend the Creational ladder and build a CORE that can exist in other realms. (Though it is important here to appreciate that there is nothing "religious" or "spiritual" about this, it is entirely a practical affair and in a sense the human is looking for "job opportunities" elsewhere in Creation.)

It is entirely possible that the preborn have, prior to their physical birth, seen something of the event into which they will be born. There is even palpable evidence that once a person acquires an identity and is looking to reincarnate, the life awaiting a new physical body has a degree of choice in selecting future parents and even that their transient line may suggest a useful choice to make.

In conclusion, as the preborn approaches its appearance in the physical world, it has an INVENTORY of content and influence, both natural and unnatural which it has gathered in its journey so far. Dependent on what has happened to it in the previous nine months, it will have strengths and weaknesses in the "hand" it has been dealt, all of which are likely to be confirmed by the physical life situation it now finds itself. It may even have pre-cognisance of its

THE LIVING EVENT OF THE HUMAN LIFE

origins before birth and some sense of what is to come – some babies do seem to have a "knowing" look about them. Whatever the case, the new life is about to embark on a physical journey which will have far-reaching consequences for its future.

Chapter 3: The Event of Term of Pregnancy- Stage Three

Conception to birth; the situation event; the transient attendances; other connections; the quickening and further development of the physical body; the Truth and Passion of Life itself; the 'Rite to Be'; lost Creational event; the 'Newbie'; initiation of being human; the installation of Being Elemental; the Occultism of the Alive to Life.

THE LIVING EVENT OF THE HUMAN LIFE

CONCEPTION

(The formation of the Physical Body, possibly already with an occupant)

The first consideration here has to be that the Planet we live on is essentially a nursery for life with millions of species looking for opportunities to be physically born, so the competition for bodies is enormous. It is an uncomfortable thought for the living, but essentially wherever there is an act of procreation there will be a large unseen audience hoping to capitalise on the situation and enter a fertilised ovum.

It is important to note here that the Planetary body is purely and simply a physical, mechanical machine waiting for a driver. It can even survive on its own when its driver is in absentia (as in a coma). Ideally, the body's occupant should be the **Entity of Self**, which has come here to initially serve the Planet's purposes and build a future for itself but the body can easily be highjacked by other life forms at various points in the pregnancy.

It is understood that for modern humans it is hard to grasp the fact that the body is purely a machine, because we live in a culture that encourages people to believe that they themselves are their body rather than its occupant. This is an inevitable consequence of living in a world which resolutely and, despite the weight of evidence to the contrary, refuses to take account of the unseen worlds. But in order to best appreciate the content of this book it is advisable to think of the body as a machine or vehicle that eventually wears out and goes to the scrap-yard, at which point if anything of the previous occupant has survived, they need to find a new physical containment.

THE EVENT OF TERM OF PREGNANCY

Do you stay in the car when you take it to the scrap yard? NO? So what happens to YOU when the vehicle of your body comes to an end?

However, to continue with the theme of Conception the reader must note that this is a prime point at which the new Creational life can enter a new form, be it human, animal, insect or whatever; however, there are other points during pregnancy when the foetus can quicken. Nonetheless, it is at Conception when the ovum (which has a powerful magnetic attraction for ALIVE) is able to be fertilised by the sperm (which is virtually an entity of ALIVE) We live at the end of history on a planet which has had a very unique and turbulent past, much of it unfortunate, and as a consequence there is a huge residue of previous lives who are looking for a body in which to reincarnate (this will be dealt with later). The reader needs to understand that today there are probably more people alive than at any point in the planet's history and everyone who has a content that has managed to survive the shock of the death of their physical body will be looking for a new embodiment; the situation would have been very different even say, ten thousand years ago, when the human population would have been far smaller.

Today the electro-magnetic realms of the Planet, which stretch as far as the **Van Allen belts**, are stacked and loaded with the

THE LIVING EVENT OF THE HUMAN LIFE

accumulated signals of tens of thousands of years of past history, much of it regrettable; in the same way, **the Human Aura**, which contains the electro-magnetic signals of the person, represents the accumulation of experience and thought process of that human and will be either fine or coarse **according to their mental processes**. (Much could be added here but it really requires another book to be written about it). Suffice it to say that what is engraved in a person's life is written in letters ten foot high in their aura for those who are able to see and sense these things and it is the same for the Planet. The electro-magnetic fields of the planet contain her history, as well as an unprecedented number of people hoping for a new shot at life and many of these will be gathering at conception and at other points in the pregnancy and hoping to enter the new life. Therefore, at conception and indeed, whenever there is sexual activity that might lead to conception, there are ATTENDANCES, some possibly from the couple's Transient tree, some from elsewhere, all hoping to seize the opportunity of life.

THE EVENT OF TERM OF PREGNANCY

THE QUICKENING

(The arrival of the new occupant)

For this reason, alongside the newly arriving Creational spawn there may well be a host of others waiting in the expanse of the planetary domains and hoping for another stab at life. Therefore, at the point of conception or quickening (sometimes even later in the pregnancy) a struggle may occur between the **"newbie"** (the newly formed entity of self) and the various attendances surrounding the pregnancy event hoping to reincarnate. Of these, those in prime position are likely to be members of the mother's own transient or family line awaiting rebirth.

After conception, if neither a person awaiting reincarnation nor a new Creational arrival (from the **Spawning**) has managed to enter the embryo, there are other points when something can get in, the **quickening** being a prime point. The ability to "home in" on a signal is a feature of all life (the migration of birds being a prime example here). Creation itself works on powerful attractions between things of kind and clearly there is a predisposition to clairvoyance, divination and sympathetic connection running in families which facilitates the attachment of a member of the woman's transient tree at this point.

The foetus will continue to grow until it is pentagrammic in shape (meaning it has four limbs and a head). Possibly, the most famous example of the human as a pentagram is Leonardo Da Vinci's Vitruvian Man, which was an attempt by the artist to demonstrate the natural laws regarding form expounded by the Roman architect Vitruvius and as it applies to man.

THE LIVING EVENT OF THE HUMAN LIFE

The **pentagram** is a high **Sun level** symbol which belongs with the human and is indicative of a higher divinity than planetary level (planetary life generally has a divinity of four, being indicative of the pedigree of something). At the moment the foetus becomes a pentagram, it is confirmed as **human**. The mother then emits a signal and something enters the developing embryo and the so-called "quickening"

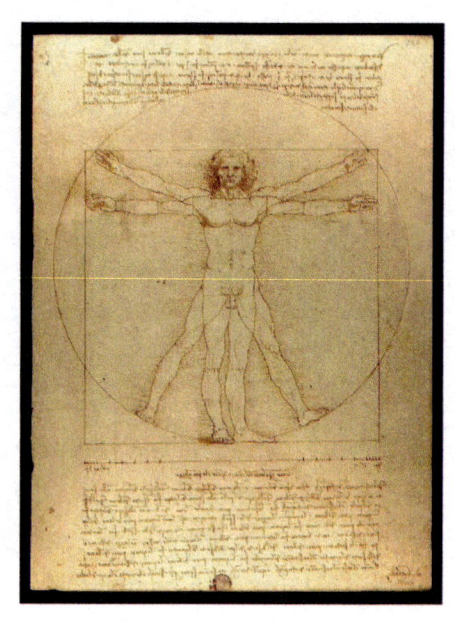

Da Vinci's Vitruvian Man

occurs. (Obviously if something already entered at conception this is no longer possible) Priority may be given to members of the mother's family tree (her transient line) if there are any available simply because of the principle of sympathetic resonance.

So, from the start, the core entity of self (which constitutes a creational issue with creational promise) can be overwhelmed by history in the shape of the woman's family tree even if it has not already been overwhelmed by general cultural input from the astral domains (for further details see Chapter 2). Furthermore, within the mother (who is simply constructing a physical machine) the foetus has to gradually occupy a space for life. Everything living radiates and generates an electro-magnetic field around itself – hence the human aura and the electromagnetic fields of the Planet herself – and these reflect the living content of the person or place. Obviously, the mother herself also has an aura. As the foetus grows it gradually occupies more space within the mother herself, both physically and electrically. As it does so the Alive in it also expands to fill the space enclosing the child; after birth this will constitute the aura of the new life.

Pregnancy gathers around the mother a series of custodial events. She herself will be sensitive to what she is pregnant with and it is important to remember that she is employed here on behalf of the Planet herself. At certain points in world history women would have been very conscious of this as a first principle. However, today the prime consideration is the indoctrination of the unborn child with the values and standards of the family and culture the mother represents. It is also important to realise that many transient trees (the family line) carry a lot of occult power and are able to block off others who do not carry the family signal.

THE LIVING EVENT OF THE HUMAN LIFE

DUTIES AND SERVICES
(Other arrivals...)

At conception, a person who is serving a specific planetary function, who has probably already reincarnated several times before or someone who is serving a high Creational purpose or duty can jump the queue because of the power of the **Alive** in them and their content. There are lives that have developed to a point where, rather than escape the Planet, they are called to do a DUTY of life that will occur within the planetary domains and assist **planetary life evolution**. Equally, all have to stand aside for a person who carries **"Way"** (see Chapter 4). It is also important to consider that there are several prime moments during pregnancy when something can get into the developing body.

The Truth and Passions of Life Itself

This most important subject seems to get lost in the hurly burly of life today where most life, human or otherwise, is struggling to survive in circumstances far from ideal. Perhaps we should then take a moment to consider the wonder of all this and spend some time dwelling on the amazing place we live and the creation in which we find ourselves appearing. The fact of life appearing here, in the face of incredible opposition and difficulty (one's own life being a case in point) should truly take one's breath away and build a resolve in self to value it and fight for it in any way one can. The fact of being born in a special place where life exists in abundance should in no way cheapen it but rather to champion it in any way one can, beginning with one's own existence.

THE EVENT OF TERM OF PREGNANCY

FROM TERM TO BIRTH

The reader needs to appreciate that although the original Creational event instigated by the Spawning has the possibility of **ascension** and a return to its source of arising, nothing that is planetary can escape the Planet. The human, being pentagrammic in shape, has a form and shape which is above planetary level (Sun level origins) and can therefore build embodiments above planetary that allow a person to rise above their planetary point of issue. This does not, however, happen automatically; it requires a lifetime of dedicated work around a self-chosen purpose to accomplish this.

The Venus of Willendorf

A person reflecting on the mysteries of pregnancy might imagine that a person's difficulties begin at birth, but in reality, they start within the mother during the journey from conception to birth. Mother and child are inextricably linked by blood (which is itself highly Occult) and the experiences of the mother can and are printed on the child, all of which can overlay and subsume the emerging self. Consequently, the newly-arrived human - who constitutes a creational event-, easily loses that creational purity – it is easy to become more

THE LIVING EVENT OF THE HUMAN LIFE

what your mother wants you to be rather than your true SELF.

It is also very important to understand that the woman and soon-to-be mother should occupy a very significant place on the Planet. The Planet herself is female (all female planets have a great deal of water on them and water is fundamental to life as we understand it). It is the female of the species that has the ability to build a new life form inside herself (obviously after fertilisation by the male). It is also why pregnancy itself may feel "special" to the woman, who is really acting as a SURROGATE for the Planet herself.

Alongside the mother's transient line, there may be other lives looking to take up the challenge of physical existence again, particularly more developed **duty or service** people that are specifically drawn to a time or place to help the Planet or the Human Race or both. The Planet herself is driven by the need for the right quality of **PRODUCE** that will serve her purposes rather than the gratification of sex or even the local idea of "I want a baby"- the Planet has her eye on her own evolution and creational future and is operating on a time scale that is vastly different to that of the human and human culture. A thousand years may be a long time to us but it is scarcely a heartbeat to the Planet.

To continue this theme, it was the recognition of the high significance of the female on this planet that lay behind matriarchal societies in past epochs; not only did these give recognition to the unique connection between women and the Planet, they would also have been directly connected to the transient trees located in the unseen worlds and themselves headed up by matriarchs.

There is evidence of matriarchal societies in American Indian tribes (where ultimately decisions were in the hands of the older women) and clearly a number of very ancient cultures revered goddesses and paid due respect to the female.

Today, the Mosuo women of China, who practise Tibetan Buddhism, appear to be the world's last surviving matriarchal society, in which, as it was with some American Indians, property is matrilineal and lineage is traced through the female line.

Mosuo Dancers

However, to return to the topic of quickening and the building of a new human form that will then occupy a space for life it is at this point, as the foetus is welded into the physical body, **the Creational Event is lost**. What is being built inside the mother now belongs to the Planet and the Solar System and the core of the person is now limited to the possibility of what the body can do. Creational event is lost at this stage because Creation Event stops at the Solar doorway and Creation can only work with Creation. **The Solar doorway** is a two-way affair and Solar can later be seen as a launching platform for a person's creational journey, should they aspire to that, but at this point the unborn child is facing the roulette wheel of planetary life rather than the proposition of building an event of self that is greater than what we are now.

THE LIVING EVENT OF THE HUMAN LIFE

FROM TERM TO BIRTH

(Further gatherings that occur prior to birth)

It is important to realise that what has been gathering in the mother has **a power of life and a rite to be** previous to its appearance as a physical life form. It has individuality and should therefore have an entitlement to freedom and the power to be itself. The rite to be oneself is upheld by the Planet and by the antiquity of the human event.

This does not include the cultural event that currently occurs on the planet (cultural meaning the current organisation of human affairs that governs life here) for **there are no rites inherent in a culture,** rites belong with **actuality.** The way we live today, although it is no one's fault because it is the result of a long history that has been inherited from our forebears, basically happens at a huge cost to the **natural worlds and the actuality of the real self.** The "rite to be" relies upon a successful end result for its confirmation and unfortunately cultural roles will not provide this – it needs a determined uptake of the true individuality of a person to satisfy creational criteria and protocols. These protocols (mentioned by John Bunyan in "Pilgrim's Progress" where he refers to the "wicket gate" that the genuine must enter through) are a guarantee to the planet and Creation that only the **right self** actually gets through.

The Creational event in physical form refers specifically to the human brain, which has a unique possibility because of its origins. Currently, the brain is mostly used minimally by the human and certainly not to its true potential. It is however, possible for the **Entity of Self** to essentially occupy the brain as a living form, in which case a whole new level of process, perception, ability and ultimately progress becomes possible for the human. (In fact, an astrophysicist at the University of Bologna and a neurosurgeon at the University of Verona compared the network of neuronal cells in the human brain with the cosmic network of galaxies with astonishing results.[1]) Essentially, the brain was not meant to be just a planetary occurrence; it has creational origins and can connect beyond the planet, if it has the right occupant.

It is also important to note that the nine-month period of formation in the womb has significant consequences for the human as it constitutes the foundation of a **cycle based on nine** that subsequently has important repercussions upon the future child and its life. This is obviously very significant and impacts upon all human life but it is not something which can be gone into in much detail here; the perceptive reader however, will note that it is a further example of the importance of studying planetary laws alongside this order of work. Suffice it to say that the first nine steps of anything are to do with **natural creational event** happening on the planet (after all, there are truly only nine numbers, all the others are a permutation of these, with the addition of zero).

The **lost Creational event** refers to the way in which, for the most part, life today is not permitted to be the age it was designed to be but is hurried through its development to satisfy the needs of culture and education. This has been the case on an increasing scale since the Industrial Revolution. (This is not to say that all children prior to this had the opportunity to experience what they were in a pure form but plainly for some a more natural experience was

---

[1] https://www.labroots.com/trending/space/19198/researchers-human-brain-shares-structure-universe

THE LIVING EVENT OF THE HUMAN LIFE

possible). Clearly, there is a cognisance and behaviour that belongs with the age a person is and each year of life needs to experience the fullness and richness that is proper to it to build the right containment for the developing self. Much of the **vitality of life** that a person is going to need is accrued here and once gone, the rightful expression of those years cannot be recovered.

THE EVENT OF TERM OF PREGNANCY

THE NEWBIE

(A first time ever appearance on the Planet consequential to local spawning)

The first consideration here is that everybody was a **"newbie"** originally, before the option to have a second life or to reincarnate and in the beginning the planet herself needed life to fulfil her purpose; today, at the end of a long and complicated history she has an abundance of life and has less need of new issue.

Furthermore, the newbie is more natural than a person who is approaching their next life or reincarnation and still has a Creational self; for this reason, the newbie doesn't experience the same order of problems as those whose creational origins lie a long way in the past.

However, the newbie is likely to struggle with the initiation of being human, because in no way is today's human creational, they have been "planetised". As a result, becoming human comes at a cost, because as they change to accommodate planetary life, they surrender that higher creational signal. It is likely that the initiation into being human will come from the child's mother and the transient tree. It is likely that in their first physical appearance here newbies feel on their own both in life and in the culture.

However, at this point, as the life makes its nine-month journey towards planetary existence and assuming that the newly manufactured person can escape the incursions of the mother's transient tree (or others who are hoping to seize the opportunity of life here), they constitute a "newbie" - that is, someone who is making their first appearance here on planet Earth, an entirely new individual who has never passed this way before. Despite their creational origins, the person has been spawned at a lesser level than Creation. The Creational Spawn will already have drifted a long way from its point of origin, bypassing constellations, clusters and stars and the higher opportunity of life there because, if we liken Creation to a ladder planetary level is almost the bottom rung. The Solar System is the smallest living unit in a Creational event, exactly like a single cell in the human body. This particular solar system is a rather special one in that it has the possibility of creating other solar systems (in the same way as a single cell can divide and produce a facsimile of itself). However, not to digress too much, for at this point it is important to consider **the initiation of being human**.

As a consequence of the high divinity of the human design (the pentagram being the badge of high Sun level divinity) humans have the possibility of building Sun and Solar embodiments in themselves that act as a platform for higher existence. However, it must be noted that this is not automatic, it is something a person has to dedicate their lives to and it is not something this particular culture is geared towards (though there have been very advanced cultures in the past for whom this was the driving motivation.)

The starting point for the new life is planetary and from the Planet's point of view it is intended to be a functional working part of the system; in order to make the necessary Creational connections one has to become HUMAN and regrettably many thousands of years of deviant history has displaced much of the natural technology which should have been the human birth right. So many human abilities– such as being divinatory, being able to see the unseen worlds, being able to connect to elementals, earth life and other extraordinary things – have been relegated to the realms of the fanciful, the eccentric or downright foolish. As a consequence of the way human life has, over the millennia, not just drifted but virtually sprinted away from **planetary purpose** and the **"rite to be"** as the Planet and Creation intended, the **"initiation of being human"** is something we have to work towards. Unlike the other flora and fauna of Earth which is awake to its natural purpose of life and is WHAT IT IS (they can only be as they were designed to be), humans have a journey to make back to the ACTUALITY of themselves and WHAT they are. However, it is likely that the unborn child, if a "newbie", is likely to be closer to the ACTUALITY of being human than a person who is repeating a previous life or looking to reincarnate.

Nonetheless, the new life will spend nine months encased within the mother (its physical maker) being initiated to a degree into what it means to be human and what it means to have an elemental outplay.

Installation of Being Elemental happens through the Planet herself; the newbie has already been given some elemental and it is certainly true that "to get gold you must first have some gold yourself". It is certainly true that young children often have a great deal of natural connection both to elemental and earth life realms (witness the age-old childhood fascination with so-called "fairy stories" and the number of children who talk about unseen friends – it is reported that up to sixty percent of children between the ages of three and eight talk about a so-called imaginary friend). It is important that the reader understands that the elemental aspect of a person is to do with their outward expression; the BEING aspect of humans is to do with their inner life or core. This is perhaps the place to give an initial explanation of the relationship between the Being life and the Elemental life and the vital part it plays in our human lives.

THE LIVING EVENT OF THE HUMAN LIFE

To continue our exploration of the human relationship and its natural surroundings, to a degree and in despite of the drift away from Planetary Purpose, the unborn child will be to a certain extent "wired-up" to the Planet herself and her purposes. It is the Planet that provides the signal that makes the heart beat ("heart" does actually anagram to "earth") and the young child is quite likely to have a particular affinity with Nature from the start of their physical life. This would have been very much the situation in antiquity before the planetary purposes were overwhelmed by history and wrong manufacture. "Newbies" are comparatively rare today due to the enormous demand for new bodies by millions of pre-existent lives, but they in particular are likely to have a freshness and innocence about them which is easily recognisable by those that are able to see.

Finally, one must consider the **Occultism of the Alive to Life**, occult here referring to the unseen and hidden potential of the Alive. The Occult here should be understood as the great power of the rite of life previously spoken of; everything in nature contains a great deal of kinetic power that is to do with its point of origin – the word "occult" unfortunately has sinister connotations in our culture but in truth there is nothing sinister in the power that drives a seed to grow and reach towards the light.

Part of the intention behind this book is to develop a more profound and actual understanding of words that are quite loosely banded about in our world. As an example, it is important to understand that qualities of living that are spoken of very loosely in our current culture such as spirituality and love actually refer to very high Creational entities that can only appear here as a fuel because for them to appear as the WHAT of themselves would be damaging to the Planet. For this reason, Alive turns up here as living rather than as its more potent source, which is not to say that the human cannot come closer to this very powerful Entity as they grow and develop. Indeed, it is vital that anybody wishing to become the Entity of Self in truth must aim to be Awake, Conscious and Alive.

Chapter 4:
First Physical Life

CONSIDERATIONS: FROM BIRTH TO THE BODY'S END. FIRST LIFE

The first consideration has to be that at birth humans find themselves born on a single planet within a solar system. In addition, they are one type of species amongst many; every life form is limited to a species time of life and living. All physical life form and shape is fixed; there is a range within it but humans can't naturally opt to grow horns!

The next consideration is that upon this planet the Natural Laws, Criteria and Protocols of life hold all life itself in Obeyance; the consequences of falling off a thirty-foot building are dire, unless you happen to be a bird or have wings – you will immediately succumb to the Law of Gravity! In addition, all species of planetary life are connected to the planet itself; they have their origins here and would not, without artificial support, be able to live on the Moon or Mars.

The third consideration is that all life requires nourishment and energy, so everything must eat to live, grow and survive. On this planet, all life breaks down into the form of herbivore or carnivore and must eat to survive; one only has to take a detailed look at food webs and chains to see this is the case – blackberries feed greenfly which are in turn eaten by sparrows which are in turn eaten by sparrow hawks and so on.

Life here is cyclic and seasonal, witness the changing seasons, the migration of birds and wildebeest, even the biorhythms in the

THE LIVING EVENT OF THE HUMAN LIFE

human body. All life here has the promise to prosper and proliferate; even the Bible tells us, "Go forth and multiply"!

In further considering the conditions of life here at planetary level, all planetary life is indisputably self- reproducing by gender. Planetary life must first be conceived by the parent mother and all species can only reproduce their own specie. The higher the specie the more the individual decision of pregnancy (and the more nurtured the offspring rather than cast willy-nilly to take its chance in the world!) All life forms have a distinct and mostly different time or term of pregnancy, geared towards the optimum chances of survival, hence the frenzy of procreation in Spring in so many species. With regard to length of gestation, it ranges from puppies (viable from 55 days) to nine months in humans and horses to a staggering twenty-two months in elephants!

The more primitive the species appearance at birth the more nurturing the mother needs to be if the offspring is going to survive: in dogs, the newly whelped puppies can't even defecate or urinate without stimulation from their mother, nor can they regulate their body temperature. So, in higher animals it is essential that the mother feels a powerful bond with her progeny at least at first. It is interesting that prey animals such as horses or wildebeest are able to run within moments of birth. For many species, being part of a family or tribe (a collective) is essential to survival.

Humans are born in a physically limited and helpless condition and urgently require the support of the mother for a very long time if they are to survive so it is essential that the mother continues to feel powerfully connected to the child long after having given birth. Also, the values and events the mother has experienced during pregnancy are likely to be upheld and confirmed by the ecology the child now finds him or herself growing up in.

Equally, humans are different by gender and, although in some parts of the world some parents are becoming more fluid about the stereotypes that are associated with gender in the vast majority of cultures, even today, there are established conventions about the different ways boys and girls are treated which are very difficult to circumvent.

Looked at from the standpoint of planetary purpose and actuality, all things feminine are close to the planet because she is herself feminine and, were the world in a natural condition this would be reflected in the respect accorded to women. Equally, just as women are the representative of the Planet, men are ambassadors for the Sun, which represents the masculine, and were things as they should be, there would be an accord between the genders that mirrors the accord and working partnership of planet and sun. There is little doubt that there have been cultures on the Planet in antiquity that were based on exactly those high principles and standards.

In the first twenty-four hours after birth what has happened between the baby and the mother continues to take place, the difference being that it now occurs "wirelessly". This is unquestionably the case with many species including humans. There is also a difference between genders here in that it takes longer for the female child to distance herself from the mother than the male, unquestionably because of the strong empathic links between mother and daughter.

It is highly likely that the "newbie" (assuming that this first life has originated from the constellational spawning) finds themselves born into a world in which the Transient Tree of the mother is the overweening influence. The Transient Tree is essentially the family line that stretches back through millennia to the distant origins of the human race. At the head of it sit the matriarchs, in the astral or ethereal realms, whose purpose is to be part of the advanced higher human race that the Planet will need when she herself becomes a star. These purposes are obviously not up front in the average family, but they are nonetheless very real. Clearly, not all transient lines will make the grade in terms of evolutional promise (though there is clearly a long way to go before this is an actuality for the Planet); many have already died out, some have been almost entirely culturized and some have reached a point where the Planet has taken them to her core and crystallised them – but for the majority of newbies the standards, attitudes and behaviour of their immediate family is going to be the mainstay of their future lives. This is very important to understand as this first life is the foundation for all future lives, and if the person crystallises in a way that is not useful it will require great efforts to undo that process. Moreover, if the person's future lives also occur within the same family tree it is likely that unfortunate processes are simply re-confirmed. (Looking at well-verified cases of reincarnation, it is interesting to note how many children who have a clear recollection of previous lives believed themselves to be a deceased relative).

Immediately after birth, the child's transient line carried by the mother's DNA together with the influence of cultures from antiquity continues to impact on the child. The transient line is particularly interested in the event, especially if the new child is female, because this represents new custodianship of the future for the family tree. It is interesting that many people on their death bed talk about seeing relatives gathered around them (who are unseen to everyone else). This is also often the case at the time of birth and immediately after when there may be a large unseen attendance from the family tree, both the unborn and the physically alive. This is hardly surprising as the new arrival represents an unknown future.

At the same time, the Planet herself has master-ship over the physical life emotions of the mother and child, not only through the term of pregnancy but from birth and for the first years. It is obviously very important that for many species, including human, it is essential that the mother and offspring are closely bonded and the Planet herself has an interest in this.

Not forgetting that we are talking here of the first physical life and the newbies first experience of the planetary world, it is necessary to note the importance of the mother's desires for the child. Today cultural indoctrination can occur at a very young age; indeed, some wealthy and ambitious parents even select the school of their choice for **their offspring** prior to birth. A person born into a royal or aristocratic family will probably already have their future mapped out for them. Furthermore, there will be constraints of income and possibly caste that will further determine the new life's future. Today in the West children have a compulsory education promulgated by society via teachers, advisors and counsellors and this will also drive the newbie into a particular direction.

Other considerations include the use of surrogates – though now a feature of modern life, this practise is very ancient, for the Bible tells us that Abraham and Sarah were unable to have a child so Sarah turned to her servant Hagar to carry Abraham's son. Today surrogacy is normally contracted and there is a whole raft of legislation governing this but in the past it was often enforced – consider the slave owners who found it cheaper to breed their own slaves than to buy them.

It is commonly understood that humans have for generations

endeavoured to breed to type with respect to animals, aiming to produce a specie that suits their own purposes. What is less often remarked upon is the degree to which transient lines try to control their own breeding with a view to influencing future generations in a particular direction. Historically, children have been contracted to other children and in Tudor times marriage via a proxy could be arranged if the children were too young. Clearly such marriages carried a political agenda in which the children were merely pawns in the bigger game. Arranged marriages are still very common today especially in India. No doubt parents are usually trying to find a partner that will bring happiness to their child, but they are also endeavouring to guarantee a specific future for their family line. Indeed, many so-called "honour killings" appear to occur when a young person tries to go against the family wishes and marry someone deemed unsuitable. At certain points in history this endeavour to guarantee certain qualities has gone completely wrong, as in the declining days of Ancient Egypt when incestuous relationships undertaken to maintain pure blood lines were the order of the day. The Pharoah Tutankhamun was a case in point as he is believed to be the product of a relationship between Akhenaton and one of his own sisters; modern x-rays of the Pharoah's mummified body show him to have a club foot. Tutankhamun also married his half-sister and as the union was without progeny the line then died out.

A more modern example is Charles II of Spain (06/11/1661-01/11/1700) who as part of the Hapsburg dynasty which took marrying within the extended family (prevalent in many of the Royal houses of Europe) to extremes with out of eleven Spnaish

Portrait of Charles II of Spain by Juan Carreño de Miranda

marriages two were between uncle and niece and one of those were his parents; as a consequence he had numerous health issues and if you notice on this portrait the well-known Hapsburg protruding jaw.

PHYSICALITY

(Coming to terms with living in a physical body)

In the first physical life, the person (having come from the rarefied electro-magnetic realms) now finds themselves living in a physical body which can suffer pain and has definite limitations in terms of what it can actually do. Also, as the human body is a particularly complex machine, it takes a long time to gain mastery over it. Life in a physical body is a very different experience than life in the astral or ethereal realms. The human body is a marvellous machine with skills and abilities that are far beyond those of other planetary life forms. However, it clearly has limitations and eventually, it wears out. It also takes human life far longer to grow and mature than any other planetary life form; the human brain is not fully "wired-up" until at least the mid twenties.

In the first physical life the person should be close to their natural origins and able to establish a connection to the close self (the real entity of self) that they started out with. At the same time, they are struggling to grow into their new machine and establish themselves in it as master or mistress of the house. All this is happening within a family or cultural environment which, through no fault of their own, is entirely oblivious of the bigger picture.

Moreover, the real Self stands in its own space and it stands alone; the newbie will be much more aware of this and the feelings attendant on it than those of us who have already experienced several lives and are more distant from the entity of self. The feelings of the close self begin with the true nature of the person but they can change as a consequence of cultural life and identity and personification may take over. On the one hand, there is the natural and connected core of the person; on the other hand, there is the undeniable fact that whatever you do in your life you will have to spend some time in a role. If that role is particularly consuming, then it can overwhelm the core of the person and stand in the place of the core self. An easy to grasp example of this is that of a person who becomes a priest, in which case the real self is likely to be overwhelmed by everything attendant on that ideology.

The new person clearly has connections and endowments from their origins including the life form they now occupy but, unfortunately, they now find themselves in a circumstance which is unlikely to allow these to flourish. However, the high pedigree of the human form does mean that they have many assets at their disposal, including a head domain that is superior to that of most other planetary lives. It is by making a full use of the incredible human possibility that a person is able to eventually recover the lost connections to the natural self and regenerate them. Whether or not the person is able to do this will depend upon their mental and emotional stance and conditioning, and also the purpose and degree of motivation that drives them. As James Allen said, "the world stands aside for the man who knows where he is going."

However, if the person is fortunate, they will manage to retain something of their original and natural self, particularly if they are able to build on their natural connection to the planet and her ways. The planet has her own purposes and agenda (explained elsewhere) and will be drawing the life to natural strengths, abilities and connections locked inside the human complex itself. This is perhaps the place to point out that at no point in the cycle of re-appearance here are there guarantees and many lives simply don't make it. It is in this first life, the life of a "newbie" that there is the highest failure rate. It is easy to see that the natural worlds work according to definite rules and criteria; a daffodil, a calf, a kitten, everything has certain design features that they have to conform to – indeed in the natural world some animals will instinctively refuse to suckle offspring which they instinctively feel is not right. Also, there must be a certain amount of luck involved – like the plant seed that is just right, but drifts on to stony ground where it can't grow.

FIRST PHYSICAL LIFE

THE NEAREST CULTURE

(The inevitability of finding oneself born
into a culture/a collective)

Wherever the new life finds themselves there will be a culture already in attendance. Even the transient tree itself is a culture because all families have their own required behaviours and protocols and wherever a collective of people occurs, culture inevitably follows. As far as the new child is concerned the culture of the transient tree is the most easily recognisable because of its proximity to their life.

The first life is full of problems because it can't express the natural life of self. How it expresses itself is determined by the tramway to expression that the culture it finds itself in makes use of. This is unlikely to be very close to the natural criteria of the Planet and Creation. On the contrary, it is likely to be governed by the dogma and sociology of the culture itself.

Therefore, there is bound to be a divergence between the original purpose of the new life and the purposes and intentions of the culture it finds itself immersed in. The true what you are requires all of you to be a viable entity and it is extremely unlikely that it will survive intact as an actuality in the world as it stands today. This is why the option for a second life and subsequent reincarnations has evolved here, in order to give the first life the opportunity to salvage their lost or fragmented self and re-engage with the human possibility.

To sum up, when considering the situation of the new life, we live in a culture which has its own aims and intentions and which, of necessity, take up a great deal of a person's time and energy. For this reason, there is likely to be an ongoing tussle between the natural inclinations of the child, reinforced and upheld by the planet, and the demands of the culture they live in, reinforced by their family, their nation and the demands of the time they live in. Today's culture is particularly virulent in that it is a media culture which has insinuated itself into the furthest and most remote parts of the planet – even Eskimos and Bedouin tribesmen appear to have mobile phones – whereas a hundred years ago it was probably still possible to meet an Amazon tribe whose way of life was untouched by the prevalent culture and still lived simply and in harmony with the Planet, it is now quite impossible.

It is worth remembering that whenever a person appeared in history, they appeared within a culture, be it Ancient Egypt, an Aboriginal tribe, a Japanese samurai family or a Scottish clan. They also appeared at a particular time, in a particular period and the expectancy of their family and culture would be that they conform to it. Therefore, the young life is likely to be corralled into a particular personality or self- expression by the expectancy of culture and within that confinement and realm of behaviour there may be little room for the natural expression of the true self. This is why the new life finds itself on a tramway of expression laid down by cultural and family expectations that it is very difficult to circumvent or escape from.

Today we have a mass education process in the West which is intended as "the engine of our economy", "the foundation of our culture", and "an essential preparation for adult life". (Nick Gibb, Schools Minister addressing the Educational Reform Summit 2015). None of this relates to the emancipation of self or planetary or creational purpose.

As a consequence of this, there will inevitably be a divergence between the actual entity of self originally spawned in a person and what it was predicted to become and the condition it might find itself in at the end of life. It is therefore hardly surprising that there is a sixty percent failure rate for lives making the difficult journey towards themselves.

Without making a deep study of natural law, it is very difficult to predict what a person might have been if they had been born into a world which allowed the natural self to flourish. What can be said is that by the end of the first life some remnants of the original self may still exist and may get through into the next life. Much of the original promise of life will have suffered entropy and will require restoration in a future existence.

TRANSIENCE

(Further explanation of the pervasive influence of the transient line)

· The newbie runs with a tendency to be natural; during the pregnancy the mother is usually very divinatory and this may well impact on the child. All newbies are connected to the astral domain of the Planet and are sensitive to their core and origins. Everything is born with a pedigree and caste and that of the newbie is creational in the first place. The whole point of life is to avoid everything that isn't you but, as has been remarked before, the newbie has to struggle with the restrictions of culture and the family tree – clearly, hereditary has its own culture and the divinatory abilities of the newbie are likely to start with those closest to it, that is relatives.

Divination comes very naturally to the newbie because it is a standard planetary ability – it stretches from clairvoyance, to empathy, to mediumship, to sensitivity to psyche and beyond and is part of the human birth- right. Obviously like everything it requires practise and the more a person practises the more they develop the skill, whatever it is. By the end of the first life some newbies are very divinatory, providing an excellent platform for the persona they need to develop for the growing entity of self.

Alongside all of this, there are clearly influences and persuasions in the background of the life that stem from that person's life as a "newbie". These may include the influence of family (perhaps the person came from a strong farming line where generations have worked the land and have a strong affinity with a particular place), the effect of religion (there are families who have cleaved devotedly to a particular faith for hundreds of years for whom marriage outside that faith is anathema) and the nature of the family themselves. Just as an experienced person can look at the pedigree of a particular litter of puppies and, by studying the parents and their forebears, have a fairly accurate understanding of the physical traits of the offspring and, more importantly, **their offspring**, it must be possible to see something of the content of a family line.

Perhaps there is a strong inclination towards the arts – for example the Bach family produced fifty known musicians and several notable composers, of which Johan Sebastian Bach was the most famous. It is tempting to conclude that in cases like this it is a content that is reappearing rather than the actual person.

Portrait of JS Bach by Elias Gottlob Haussman

THE LIVING EVENT OF THE HUMAN LIFE

THE EMERGENT SELF

(The fulfilment of the original promise of life)

It is important to realise from the start that each individual person has a unique entity of self which is really them which existed at their inception before their physical appearance on earth. This constitutes a coming together of certain powerful influences which have been described elsewhere. This unique entity needs to develop an identity, which can be thought of as a brilliant theatre in which the unique abilities of that person – including being divinatory, seeing or sensing auras, and much more – can be played out while the person is on the planet, to the benefit of both. Unfortunately, the likelihood is that the person ends up clothing themselves exclusively in a series of life roles - such as that of solicitor, doctor, dentist, policeman, politician- that they need to earn a living here. This is not to say that there is anything wrong with these roles – where would we be without doctors, dentists or policemen – but the trouble comes when they become all- consuming and leave little time for the real person locked up inside to develop.

The optimum life is the life in which a person takes possession of the REAL I AM, rather than spends their time consumed by a series of transitory roles which may build a content that is not truly compatible with the genuine person. Sadly, there are people who give their lives in totality to their career (often with no personal choice in the matter as they have a gladly embraced duty to support their family) only to feel lost and bewildered when they face retirement and no longer have that role to play. Everyone knows people who are like this. Agreed, every adult has responsibilities – to family, friends, the workplace – but they also have duties to themselves, to realise the actuality of them and to develop their own potential.

It is true that the word "duty" has fallen out of favour in today's world – it was an indelible feature of life a few hundred years ago – and people are more often likely to talk about their "rights" but surely in a balanced world both are important. Humans are part of society, part of the ecology, part of Nature herself and therefore need to take responsibility for the consequences of their behaviour; this is becoming increasingly apparent and people are starting to realise that things like recycling and global emissions impact all. Perhaps at a later date people will realise that their thought processes are equally infectious. So, duty simply means what is owed, to one's immediate family and friends, to the planet, to the future, to oneself.

THE LIVING EVENT OF THE HUMAN LIFE

PRACTICES OF LIFE

(How culture and the time in which a person lives impacts on the Self)

In considering the life of the entity of self, a person needs to consider the backdrop of the culture and times in which they live. Unless they are extremely lucky, the demands of living are likely to take away from their natural inclination. Schooling and education may be a necessary enforcement that will enable a person to earn a living and survive in the modern world but in many ways, they are unlikely to greatly assist in the emancipation of the true self. Nonetheless, the ability to read and write, to understand numbers and to have a broader understanding of the world is unquestionably vital in the realms of higher education and simply can't be dismissed.

However, by the time a person leaves school, though they may be well-equipped for cultural life and the world of work, they may already feel distanced and cut off from their real selves. They may feel dissatisfied, at odds with themselves, restless and already questioning the direction their life is going in. In time, this may lead to an interest in religion, philosophy or even a cult which promises to help them "find themselves". The problem here is that mostly what is available offers the balm of belonging to a collective (offering group identity); this may offer solace and comfort to some but it is unlikely to nourish the quest in a person to uncover the uniqueness that is them – like the Borg in Star Trek, they are much more likely to be absorbed in the collective! Although science fiction ideas such as the Borg or Doctor Who's "Cybermen" are fictional, it is interesting to note the instinctive revulsion humans feel at the prospect of losing their individuality – no one "volunteers" to be a

Cyberman or a member of the Borg, everyone fights tooth and nail against it!

GREATER WORKS

(The times people live in - a greater picture)

Whatever epoque a person is born into there will be dominant trends at play and the individual will have to ride those trends and meld with them – it's no use behaving like a medieval person in the twenty first century and for the most part that would be impossible. Equally there are clearly times when something monumental is sweeping the planet, such as the Renaissance or the Industrial Revolution, and at these times great change can occur, not necessarily for the better. It could be argued that these turbulent times issue from life on the planet responding to the tides of Creation; it is easy to forget that the earth is not an independent nodule but part of the great moving, changing system of Creation without which nothing could exist. Historians and academics speak of the "zeitgeist" or spirit of the age as if it merely relates to what is happening in the human world but events such as the advent of say Christianity, Islam, or the origins of Ancient Egypt almost certainly resulted from human beings responding to issues from outside the planet.

So, a person wishing to pursue their unique identity will need to be very aware of the time in which they are born and its trends, because the time a person lives in will undoubtedly help shape their character.

If a person is driven by the quest for self, even unconsciously, at some point in their life they may well become a searcher. If Religion or Philosophy fails to provide satisfactory answers, they may start to delve into the Esoteric and the Occult and this may lead them to so-called secret societies such as the Masons, the Rosicrucians or the Illuminati. For some these have an attraction because they have a long history and an apparent pedigree and some humans tend to be more trusting of things that are traditional rather than the new. Equally, it is entirely possible that somewhere in their transient line they have a family association with one of these organisations. Later, possibly in a second physical life or reincarnation, it becomes likely that the person has already come across these groups previously. For centuries certain secret societies have claimed to have the answers to the deeper questions of life, but it is important to consider whether these answers have become dogmatised and fixed rather than attached to the live vitamins and influences that gave birth to them in the first place.

THE WAY

(The map to genuine self-fulfilment against the backdrop of Planetary Law)

Throughout history, there has been a means to discover one's true self which speaks of a pathway to self- discovery that begins here on this planet and does genuinely lead to something **real and actual**. In the past it was taught in the inner temples of Egypt, John Bunyan referred to it covertly in "A Pilgrim's Progress" (though the prejudices of his time forced him to dress his story up in Christian doctrine) and many so-called esoteric lives, such as Cornelius Agrippa, Madame Blavatsky, Gurdjieff and others have alluded to it. It is called the **Way** and the very words immediately suggests a journey from somewhere to somewhere. It is the name given to the pathway, founded on natural and planetary law, that allows a person to build their genuine self and create an identity that matches it; it is a pathway that definitely goes somewhere and can lead to a better life here and the promise of something greater thereafter.

The ancient Chinese philosophy "the Tao" actually means **"the Way"**; central to its beliefs is the idea that both the planet and Creation work according to natural laws, which are simple, infallible and unbiased and that the key to happiness, health and well-being is a life lived according to these laws. As Benjamin Hoff wrote in his charming exposition of the Tao ("The Tao of Pooh")[1], earth was "in essence a reflection of heaven, run by the same laws – not by the laws of men". According to Lao-tse – the purported author of the

---

[1] Benjamin Hoff. The Tao of Pooh. 1982 Dutton Books. ISBN 0-525-24458-1

THE LIVING EVENT OF THE HUMAN LIFE

Tao, the more man interfered with the "natural balance" of the "universal laws" the more the harmony retreated into the distance." This profound and very important idea has been a feature of "the Way" for millennia and many people, known and unknown have championed it. As Hermes Trismegistus wrote, "As above, so below".

The North American Indians, who themselves lived lives very close to nature and whose way of life had ancient origins, maintained that sickness and ill-health came as a consequence of being disconnected from Creation and that the sick person needed to re-connect to the planet and the natural worlds to become well again.

The beauty of relying on natural law to prove things is that one doesn't have to rely on tradition, dogma or the teachings of other people; a person can go out and prove it for themself, and there is an abundance of previous lives that have in their quiet way trod this path themselves. For example, one of the key laws governing the Planet is the Law of Two; Ralph Waldo Emerson wrote abundantly about just that and a person can find numerous examples in his work (though it is also very important a person finds examples of their own). This primary Law is seen at planetary level as opposites, for example, hot and cold, birth and death, man and woman and countless other examples. A diligent study shows that in reality many examples actually refer to both ends of the same bar. The more people study and collect examples of the laws, and do their own work upon them the more they understand the actuality of how things work.

WORKS OF ENTITY

(Building an expression of self that matches the calibre of WHAT you are)

The truth is that Creation caused the Entity of Self, not human dogma, not culture, not history and only a path that starts in the natural worlds here on this planet is going to allow a person to take possession of that unique self. It may however take many lifetimes for the genuine self to emerge and it is the purpose of this book to give the reader some starting idea of how it might happen.

It is very clear from what has been spoken of so far that the expression of the genuine Entity of Self has to match up to the natural world in which it finds itself appearing. This does not mean living in a cave or off the land or refusing to wear clothes (it is understood that building the right expression for the Self has to take place against the backdrop of the culture and times we live in, and as this particular culture is virtually world-wide there is no option other than living and developing within it).

What a person has to consider is the kind of character that they need to develop and the kind of works they need to invest in if they are to build the right kind of expression for the real self. None of this would be necessary if the human race (through no fault of its own) had not deviated from its natural purpose.

This is why proponents of the Way throughout history have stressed the need to make a deep and profound study of the laws that govern the planet and have urged people to work with the laws rather than in ways that are antagonistic towards them. So, the first step of the journey is to make a deep study of the laws because any endeavour needs to be founded on actuality rather than human fancy.

Study of the laws eventually brings a person to a situation where they can prove things for themselves rather than rely on faith, belief or the creed of someone else.

Alongside this, the person wishing to take full possession of the emergent self needs to work towards recovering the full complement of natural abilities that mostly all have lost, as a consequence of the way in which we live today. This includes such abilities as being clairvoyant, psychic, divinatory, being able to see into the unseen worlds, astral travel and much more.

Obviously, all of this demands that a person undertakes a self-development journey in which they gradually re-take possession of all the natural abilities that they were born with originally but which have become dormant due to lack of usage. This is obviously much easier if one undertakes the journey alongside people who are aiming at the same goals and is virtually impossible without some guidance from someone who has already made some progress along the path.

Before moving on to the next chapter, in which we examine the pre-second life settings, it is worth pointing out there is no greater journey than that which leads to true possession of the Self and the accruing of works of entity that allow a person to be truly themselves within the great arena of the Planet, the Solar System and ultimately Creation.

Chapter 5:
Stage 5 Afterlife Stage 2

In which we examine the approach to the next physical life; the passage to reincarnation; the greater human-made life; Awakened life without Human Identity; the Reborn life (in which Content replaces Entity of Self; the Transient Lines (in which Transience conflicts with Culture); the Abandonment of Entity for Identity; End results.

AFTERLIFE TOWARDS THE 2ND LIFE AS A REBIRTH
(RE-BIRTH: THE RESET LIFE)

In a computer, a RESET clears any pending errors or events and brings the system back to its normal or initial state; therefore, the afterlife scenario here before the next attempt at life "clears the decks" as it were and makes way for a new attempt to be correct, measured against the pedigree and divinity of the human design.

When the body dies, the resultant content of the WHAT YOU ARE is measured in accordance with the natural protocols of the afterlife as instituted by planetary and creational law, rather like the Egyptian weighing of the heart against the feather of truth. Only that which is crystallised in a person is able to withstand the shock of death (Shock in the sense of a change of OCTAVE or a change of state, in that the person moves from a sense of themselves as a physical entity into the realms of electro-magnetic forces that they are actually made of).

After death, every living thing finds itself standing over its body. If a person identifies with their body (now a carcass) rather than with their own electro-magnetic CONTENT they may find it very hard to leave it. Equally, if the nature of their life has caused a thickening of the cortex or outer layer of their aura (the electro-magnetic field that surrounds the body) they may find it hard to escape their own history. (Incidentally, this is the reasoning behind the Church's last rites, which are meant to break the thickened outer skin of the aura and give the person release). It is interesting to note how, in the consideration of reincarnation, many well-verified examples of this suggest that the person who remembers a previous life has reappeared very close to the place where they died; in "Children Who Remember Previous Lives", Ian Stevenson[1] cites large numbers of Burmese who remembered being Japanese soldiers in a previous life some of who really wanted to return to Japan. The well-documented case of Bongkuch Promsin from Thailand is also interesting as he claimed to be the reincarnation of a murdered youth called Chamrat and stated that after he was murdered "he stayed on a tree near the site of his murder for about seven years" until one day "when it was raining, he saw his (present) father and followed him home on a bus". His father did remember being in that location just before his wife became pregnant.[2]

To continue, if a person has crystallised around something natural, for example WAY work, they will leave their dead body very quickly. This is also the case with planetary life forms that are natural and true to purpose. If, in the first life the person's original issue came from their mother's transient tree (lodged in the astral and ethereal realms of the planet), rather than from the purity of the Creational Spawning, this will reclaim the life immediately after death (this explains the number of dying people who claim to see dead relatives waiting for them). Even if the person standing over their dead body was a newbie in their previous life, they may have been absorbed by their mother's transient tree, having spent seventy years or more entangled in it. It is very difficult here to escape one's family line; one needs a very definite, clear purpose of life to do so.

---

[1] Ian Pretyman Stevenson (October 31, 1918 – February 8, 2007)

[2] Children Who Remember Previous Lives: A Question of Reincarnation: A Question of Reincarnation, Rev. Ed. (Revised) Paperback – 31 Mar. 2001 McFarland & Co 31 Mar. 2001 ISBN 978-0786409136   page 68

THE PASSAGE TO REINCARNATION

(In which the scene is set for perhaps many lives, ideally aimed at reconnecting to the original self rather than just subsisting)

After death, the passport to a superior opportunity in the next life is the degree to which the life measures up to the **WHAT YOU ARE**, as specified by Creational protocols and criteria; the greater the adhesion of the life to the **WHAT YOU ARE** in their previous physical appearance the better the "employment" prospects in the next scramble for a physical body. The smaller the balance of **"ACTUALITY"** – actuality being the prime currency of Creation – the lesser the job opportunities available, though the person may still have the necessary credentials for a suitable lesser or" in service" role. This at least offers the prospect of survival and the opportunity to grow in the right direction, particularly if the person can seize the opportunity of the initial **RESET** of self.

In addition, because of the great aggregate of culture recorded in the electro-magnetic realms of the planet over aeons of time, it is also feasible for a person to have crystallised a **"Cultural What"** in themselves rather than a **"Creational What"** founded on natural criteria. This occurs when someone has surrendered their life up to powerful repetitional roles such an artist, a musician or a doctor rather than the natural protocols and ways of the Planet and Creation. This will offer continuity of life but a continuity of the ROLE rather than the original **ENTITY OF SELF**.

AFTERLIFE STAGE 2

THE GREATER HUMAN MADE LIFE

(In which the Person explores the greater Possibility of Human Life)

The greater prize is the opportunity to become the Entity of Self, which equates to the original PROMISE of life as established at the time of the SPAWNING. This means the **Entity of Self**, the ACTUAL person, can occupy the higher faculties of the brain and start to develop abilities beyond those normally available to the Human.

The ELEMENTAL event of Life with its Sun and Solar origins represents a greater life with greater possibility than that of the planetary BEING and its connections. The promise of the Planetary is the "Awakened" life as demonstrated by planetary life forms such as the cat, the elephant, the fauna of earth. The promise of sun level is "conscious", which is superior to **"awakened"** with a foothold in "Animated" (Solar) (Note: planetary and sun level both occupy the **astral and ethereal domains** of the Planet, i.e., the electro-magnetic realms). Unquestionably those whose names resonate through history, the Isaac Newtons and Leonardo da Vincis of this world who have been responsible for life-changing discoveries would have been acting in response to their elemental selves.

The Greater Human Life offers the opportunity to be a self-determined Entity with a unique CORE, buttressed by a natural identity founded on the divinity and pedigree of the Human Event (as opposed to a cultural role or series of roles which are limited to a planetary appearance). It does, however, require a commitment to a

THE LIVING EVENT OF THE HUMAN LIFE

PURPOSE of life founded upon Creational Actuality and Reality. Clearly, this is a journey that can only be undertaken after much research into what is required by higher domains such as that of the Sun, Solar and beyond, and also requires that a person become open to the possibility of existence above and beyond that which we experience at planetary level. This means a person coming to terms with the fact that, even in terms of planetary cognisance, we do not have a three hundred and sixty perception of the actuality of life and without the right order of work we will never be able to grasp what it might mean to be connected to realms beyond this.

AFTERLIFE STAGE 2

TOWARDS THE 1ST LIFE AS A REBORN

(In which the Pursuit of Self is abandoned in favour of the Pursuit of Content)

The Content Life

Clearly the optimum future for the human being is embedded in fulfilment of **its Creational Purpose** and being truly aligned to its original **Entity of Self**. However, as a consequence of world history and the circumstances at play on the Planet at this time, there are unusual occurrences regarding how life happens here that are probably unique to this planet. The most striking of these is the Content Life, which happens when a person has spent their previous physical existence saturated with a particular cultural frequency, say a dedicated musician, artist or doctor, and it is this content that has crystallised in them and it and is then carried forward into their next life rather than their Entity of Self. It is worth noting here that people who are particularly close to their Elemental side are more likely to be drawn into the Reborn life as it is this aspect of self that is likely to draw them to say music or art (Remember, the Being life will draw the person to sit by a tree, the Elemental life will drive the person to climb it – famous explorers like Marco Polo, Sir Walter Rayleigh and Roald Amundsen would all have been motivated by powerful Elemental aspects of themselves).

Today, people live in a culture which is characterised by random life events which are mostly far removed from Creational Purpose. It is understood that it is not people's fault, they just pick up the gauntlet that has been handed to them by history and their family line and they do the best they can with the hand that they have been dealt. Were they born into a culture that cleaved to Creational purpose, their lives and opportunity would have been very different, but the truth is they are enrolled in a life which excludes the Entity of Self as a prime focus. For this reason, people are drawn into and become connected to containments that are connected to the long trace of history and cultural achievements and they build a powerful identity around these things rather than their genuine life. Consequently, in this afterlife (the prelude to a person's second life) they may well carry embodiments that have overlayed their previous process of living and which have more power and sway over them than their original self. They will then be seeking a new life which offers the chance to again be a soldier, or a musician or a writer. It is very interesting that some families have a long tradition of their children becoming soldiers or priests; indeed, in Medieval times it was customary for the first son in a noble family to train as a warrior and the younger son to enter the Church.

AFTERLIFE STAGE 2

AWAKENED LIFE WITHOUT HUMAN IDENTITY

(Commitment to a cause rather than oneself)

Those awaiting **REBIRTH** with the content of a previous existence have had their original life **OVERWHELMED** by a sustained singular event of life. It is this which carries **EMPOWERMENT** and is likely to have survived the shock of their physical death rather than their connection to their Entity of Self.

These people may have spent their first life in the service or practice of something else, possibly the Church (the initiated circles), or something Occult or Esoteric such as the Masons. These people may well be quite cognisant and awake, (within the limitations of their calling), in that the organisations they have served have a degree of understanding and competence at planetary level, but it is nonetheless clear that they are lining themselves up for a whole life event of slavery to a group or institution rather than to their own individual quest for self. ("Slavery" in the sense of not being their own person but belonging to something or someone else).

When the Morning Stars Sang Together
William Blake; 1820

THE LIVING EVENT OF THE HUMAN LIFE

It is interesting to note that the Planet, whose aim is to acquire a refined and elevated gathering of life forms that will assist her evolutionary journey to star level, would have a special interest in content lives of the right calibre and this would attract the attention of Planetary Life forms such as Elemental Earth Life forms (commonly known as fairies, elves, pixies and so forth) and other Elemental planetary life forms. These unseen denizens of the natural world are an essential part of the maintenance system and would unquestionably be drawn to any human making the right signal and helping the Planet acquire suitable evolutionary content for her future; it is unquestionably for this reason that great mystics like the artist William Blake clearly acquired a powerful following in the unseen worlds (in the form of nature spirits and similar), drawn to him by the fervour of his life and his commitment to his work.

AFTERLIFE STAGE 2

CONSIDERATIONS... TOWARDS THE TRANSIENT LINES

(In which we examine the conflict of Transience and Culture)

Whilst awaiting the opportunity of rebirth, the person may experience conflict between the TRANSIENT lines and Culture, not least because the higher echelons of a transient tree may be unhappy with today's culture which they may consider deviant from planetary purpose. (Remember the original purpose of the transient lines was high as it was motivated by the wish to serve the Planet and her Evolution to Star level). Hence the person may experience a heavy dominance from the Matriarchs that sit at the top of the transient tree and who demand obedience to its purposes.

The person awaiting rebirth is also likely to be surrounded by the continued intervention of their greater family (the Others) who will have their own agenda where rebirth is concerned.

The transient lines carry pedigree and caste which are derived from antiquity and beyond and would consider themselves superior to the formality of cultural control and indoctrination, which for them would be the product of a deviant culture which is lost to planetary purpose. There is also the possibility of conflict between transient lines which even stretches into not understood human behaviour as it relates to conflict between parents and children.

If a child has been reincarnated into a different family line than his own there is almost certainly going to be a conflict of ideologies that neither parent or child will understand and which is beyond the understanding of modern psychology. The young child is driven by previous experience that is beyond the comprehension of the new parent and sometimes this can be seen in precocious behaviour in the youngster which is completely alien to his new family. The child may be fierce in his determination to do something which comes from previous need but that need is quite alien and out of kilter with his present family. He may end up in a fierce struggle with a father who obviously comes from a different transient line and is immoveable in his demands and standards. This can result in a battle of wills and a complete stand-off between parent and child until a third vector (outside force) in the form of the mother comes along and breaks the deadlock and re- establishes the family norm. Clearly, this puts an entirely different complexion on the complexities of child psychology and reveals the astonishing breadth of conflicting forces and dynamics that actually govern human behaviour. It could also explain the sense in some children that they are "changelings" and that they don't belong in a particular family or even that they are "outsiders".

Issues arising from previous life experience and impacting on a child's new life can obviously be extremely important and are currently beyond the scope of modern psychology, yet, if reincarnation and rebirth is a fact of life (as credited by many religions and philosophies even today), then this is a significant aspect of many people's lives that simply goes unremarked.

AFTERLIFE STAGE 2

THE RISINGS OF ORIGIN AND PEDIGREE

(In which we reflect upon the forgotten origins of the Human Race)

It is impossible to underestimate the strength and power of the transient lines which have their origins before the Antiquity, before the Akashic[3], before the History and before the original Event in which Human Life, possibly in a very different form, began upon this Planet.

Therefore, the transient lines, which sit in the astral and ethereal realms have origins and a pedigree that is, without considerable and detailed study, quite beyond the grasp of most people. We find ourselves born at the end of a very long and troubled history which is essentially very different from the conventional story line we are all taught in school. Indeed, when Immanuel Velikovsky states in his ground-breaking book "Mankind In Amnesia" that humanity suffers from a "collective amnesia induced by global trauma", it is tempting to conclude that he is barely scraping the surface of a very different view of history which is only just being uncovered by unconventional researchers and academics. Alongside all of this, the transient lines have witnessed the Ascension of life form in a very unique way and have also watched the rising of a civilisations and cultures which were far closer to the natural event of life than we can possibly grasp.

---

[3] Wikipedia defines the Akashic records as" a compendium of all universal events, thoughts, words, emotions and intent ever to have occurred in the past, present, or future in terms of all entities and life forms, not just human."

THE LIVING EVENT OF THE HUMAN LIFE

This is admittedly difficult for most modern people to understand, for our culture tends to take the view that, as John West points out ironically in his book "Serpent In The Sky, The High Wisdom Of Ancient Egypt", "man has 'progressed'" from a very primitive state of affairs to the advanced culture of today. Accordingly, current thought takes it for granted that "There has been an 'evolution' in human affairs" and "there is nothing the ancients knew that we do not know or understand better."[4] A more enlightened view of world history would unquestionably dispute this for we live in the broken remains of high and ancient cultures that were far more advanced than our own. As John West goes on to point out" civilisation means a society organised upon the conviction that mankind is on earth for a purpose...in a civilisation, men are concerned with the quality of the inner life rather than with the conditions of day-to-day existence."

As an example, the original civilisation of Ancient Egypt, far lost in the aeons of time, was absolutely unforgiving and intolerant of anything that deviated from Maat (the personification of Creational Truth) and would have found the emancipated culture of today to be an abomination. Such a civilisation, as it sits in the transient lines and filters down the epochs, is bound to come into conflict with the modernism of culture and fashion which is far removed from a condition of natural planetary heritage. Furthermore, it is important that the reader understands that although the physical remnants of cultures like Egypt are now in decline, the unseen aspects of great civilisations live on in the astral and ethereal domains of the planet and unquestionably still exert an

---

[4] John Anthony West (September 7, 1932 – February 6, 2018) Serpent in the Sky: The High Wisdom of Ancient Egypt, Quest Books, 1979 page 6

influence today.

THE ABANDONMENT OF ENTITY FOR IDENTITY

(The embodiment and empowerment of identity over the actuality of Self)

It must be understood that at this point in the Afterlife, if a person has surrendered to either/or their transient tree or the content life of a Reborn (they could have done both simultaneously, one only has to look at musical families like that of Bach to see this) **they have abandoned the Entity of Self in favour of the pursuit of Identity**. Identity fits with a life founded upon different roles rather than the Actuality of Self though because of the peculiar and unique arrangements that exist here on the Planet identity may still carry the flush of power and control culturally. One only has to consider the cultural magnetism of the celebrity culture or the charisma of certain cultural roles (the Prime Minister, the President, the Managing Director etc) to confirm this. As a consequence of this, IDENTITY is embodied and empowered over the Actuality of Self, even though it is itself very limited in terms of future.

Reborns can also find their way into the great Orthodox or the Great Standard, as the repetitious printing of traditional religions is very fixing and can consume entire families (who may already hold this as a bias in their transient line). Again, the CONTENT of orthodox religions, all of which have occult attendance, together with a long and bloody history, can and probably will overwhelm the Actuality of Self. It must be remembered that although those who founded the world religions might have been pure in intent and might genuinely have wanted to help the Human Race, for the most part the net result has been twisted ideologies that bear little or no relationship to the original message. Moreover, REBORNS today may find themselves within orthodox religions which are challenged by dwindling standards and are subsequently shored up with on the one hand, extremism or, on the other, extreme liberality. The evidence today is that everything – from transient lines to the giant edifices of religion – are starting to fracture and breakup.

AFTERLIFE STAGE 2

CONSIDERATIONS... END RESULTS

(Continuation to 2nd Re-boot - the 2nd Physical Life)

After this roller-coaster ride, the reader may be forgiven if they have forgotten that the person concerned here is still in the electromagnetic realms of the planet hoping for a chance to be born again! Throughout this time, they are diminishing in content, because without a body one is unable to sustain oneself – there are no cafes in the Astral Light!

In the Afterlife, it is likely that those who are cognisant are likely to recognise the deficiency (meaning shortfall from original purpose) that has occurred within them, before they are once more able to engage in a physical life. It may also be that a person reacquaints with the "Way" in the sense of reawakening to the original purposes of life and the promise of the Entity of Self; in this sense, it is rather like a computer "reboot" when all the computer's logic is reset and unnecessary programmes are deleted. In a person, broken links and ties may be repaired in the same way as a computer is reset back to its factory settings.

Living as we do in a physical body which has limitations, it is difficult to appreciate that once unencumbered by physical life what is important to a person changes – they are likely to be much more cognisant of the deficiencies within themselves. They may well be looking for opportunities to change when they re-engage with physical existence.

So, the person is now looking to find a suitable body to enter in order to re-embark on their physical journey. In a sense they are

THE LIVING EVENT OF THE HUMAN LIFE

looking for a "pit-stop" to refuel, its as pragmatic as that; they may only need a short life, sufficient to regenerate and continue in the quest to stay alive. Some may even be looking for an "ending life" that is actually seeking erasure because sadly, there are some lives that don't want to live.

If a person has not been pursuing the Entity of Self as their mission of life, then they are essentially looking for a life that offers a suitable "role" for continuance. Unfortunately, there are those who have moved beyond the point where they have sufficient "points" to fuel a human body, and they may have to opt for an animal, a bird or even an insect in their desperation to keep living. This constitutes a "last resort" but the person may by this stage have diminished to the point where they have no further options available. There will be for the person a sharp contrast between what is available and what is possible with diminished remains.

It must be pointed out here that the Planet (and Creation) are the great economists and discovered "recycling" long before any human thought of it! In Pilgrim's Progress by John Bunyan (a very esoteric book cleverly disguised as a Christian guide to salvation) mention is made of "Topeth" which anagrams to "the pot"- Pilgrim is desperate not to fall into "Topeth" with the weight of his burden.[5] The Planet wastes nothing and wrong manufacture, ego and hypocrisy are recycled in "the pot" and probably end up on the Moon, which is young and growing and requires the right electrical impressions to do that.

It is worth pointing out here that although much is sifted and

---

[5] The Pilgrim's Progress from This World, to That Which Is to Come . 1678 Christian allegory. John Bunyan

sorted in this first Afterlife, the determining factor of what is to happen to a person has already occurred in their first PHYSICAL life. The consequences of the thoughts, the actions, the processes that someone has experienced in their past life are crystallised and become the "ticket" to their next physical appearance. It is a sobering thought but it is worth considering that it is possible "to write one's own ticket" rather than just accept the ride one is given.

Chapter 6:
Column 6: The Second Physical Life

In this chapter we examine the second physical appearance on Earth. This includes the strong sense and recall of the first life; the Reborn life (a life of containment rather than re-connection to the Entity of Self); Elemental and Earth Life involvement; developing a pedigree or caste of Content.

THE CONSIDERATIONS OF REBIRTH

The Strong Second Life Pulling to The First (the shadowy influence of the first life)

In their second physical life, the person may well carry a strong sense and recall of their first life; in their early life, they may even carry strong, up-front memories of their previous time, especially if that life ended violently. From very young, the child may have strong and clear interests which have carried through from a past life; there are even some who have nightmares based on previous existence, although it does seem that memories fade by the time the person is about six or even earlier – no doubt because of the pressing need to engage with their new life and to get to grips with the culture and family they now find themselves in.

The young child may also have a tendency to create or associate with odd friends (who are invisible to everyone else); this could well be indicative of past life experience filtering through to their present existence. Culture today has a tendency to think the new-born child is like a blank sheet of paper waiting to be written on but the truth is that the paper already carries faint marks, like invisible ink that only needs the right stimuli to be activated.

As a consequence of the shadowy influence of the first life, the person may face struggles in themselves that actually stem from a previous physical existence (hardly surprising since they may well have "unfinished business" carried over from their first life, especially if they need to undo previous mistakes). If the first life had been a complete success, they would not be returning for a second attempt

THE LIVING EVENT OF THE HUMAN LIFE

at life, as they would already have fulfilled the promise of human and started on an ascensional way. (However, given the challenging circumstances we currently find ourselves in at the end of a difficult planetary history, this could only occur if the "newbie" had been fortunate enough to come into prolonged contact with someone who was heavily immersed in "the Way" and this means that this life bypass is extremely rare). So, on the one hand, aspects of the first life may turn up as undeveloped or unwanted uncertainties or fears; on the other hand, the person may have an inner sense of knowing what to do next. This may turn up as an inner determination to follow a particular career (e.g., a soldier, a pilot, a housewife, even a nun as an example) and it may happen at a time in life when the child is really too young to make such a decision.

Obviously, the quality of the life is directly dependent upon what has managed to survive the first physical life; there is fierce competition for the right kind of Second Life and some may have only just "made it through" to a Second Life, whilst others may have opted for a life of struggle to undo previous mistakes. For others this may be an "ending" life, either because they no longer want to live, or because they have already been very successful in the building of the WHAT of them and are about to move beyond planetary to higher realms.

Whatever their personal situation, the person may well experience the awkward transposition of the secret, hidden part of themselves and the culture they now find themselves in. This may even turn up as a fascination with the period in history they were previously born in and one does wonder what draws such large numbers of people to re-enactment societies like the Sealed Knot! Equally, the person may take up a specific system for life, such as a religion or cult, entirely unaware that they already surrendered themselves to the same thing previously. Unfortunately, (or perhaps fortunately, it depends upon what you are), death and the experiences of the afterlife seem to by and large wipe memory of a previous life and only faint hints of it filter through. Furthermore, no matter what is coming through from previous existence, the Second Physical Life will come under the auspices of a Transient Tree which the person will either reject or be captured by. Even if the new person belonged previously to a different family line, they are likely to spend the formative years of their new life immersed in the behaviour, beliefs, standards and values of their present parents, all of which is likely to be a reinforcement of their experience prior to birth inside their mother.

THE CONSIDERATIONS OF REBORN – THE NEW EVENT OF LIFE WITHIN CONTAINMENT

This section principally deals with those whose re-connection and containments relate to a previously established CONTENT rather than those who have been pursuing a quest founded on the WHAT of them. People who are REBORNS will not experience past memories because what has continued from a previous life is CONTENT rather than IDENTITY.

This CONTENT may relate to any role or pursuit of life that the person previously surrendered to; this will be locked inside the inner life of the person and though it may be apparent at a very early age for some (Mozart, as an example, who was clearly a REBORN within the sphere of music and was composing music at the age of six, completed his first symphony at about nine) others may have to search in order to re- connect. For some, this may be assisted by the fact that they have stepped away from their original transient tree and chosen a more rightful family to be born into – for example, a reborn with musical content may have specifically chosen to be born into a musical family, a former soldier may have selected a family with strong ties to the military and so on.

The second physical life will automatically allow a reborn to develop even greater ability within their chosen specialism and the doing of this will turn up in them as a COMPULSION – a "can't stop themselves" EVENT. They will do exactly what they did before but much earlier and they will gravitate to those who share the same art or content; clearly those whose centre of gravity is a specific area send out a very strong signal which others of kind will be drawn to, one only has to look back in history to see this is the case, with whole schools of artists – the Pre-Raphaelites or the Impressionists as an example- gathering together to explore the same interests. The other feature of these people is their inability to adapt satisfactorily to the culture they find themselves in. From an early age, they probably feel as offset to the culture in which they are born as "Way" people and it is hardly surprising that many of these people are thought of as complete misfits even when their genius is recognised. William Blake, the great poet and artist, was described as "an unfortunate lunatic" by his contemporaries and eventually believed himself to be mad, so often the fate of those who do not follow the acceptable cultural pathway.

REBORNS experience accelerated learning and ability because they are building on a previous content rather than starting from scratch. They are often very driven people; one only has to look at history and the compulsion to succeed against often almost impossible odds that drove people like Leonardo da Vinci and Michelangelo to appreciate this. Indeed, the drive in Michelangelo to re-connect to the purity and simplicity of classical sculpture (in defiance of the trends of his time) suggests that he himself was a reborn from antiquity.

The feature of these people is that they never give up, they are driven by a deep need to excel and out do their previous best as a matter of personal principle. Michelangelo worked feverishly up until his death, desperately struggling with failing faculties and a weakening body; Beethoven (another social misfit) composed his greatest work after he became completely deaf. People like these, often REBORNS, pursue excellence in their chosen field often at the expense of their own health, family, friends and even sanity and the likelihood is, in their next life they will do exactly the same, turning up in their next physical reincarnation as an infant prodigy.

Obviously, not all REBORNS are going to appear in the realms of the Arts (though this is often a good place to look for them); someone who has had a previous life dedicated to a specific role or function – such as a counsellor, a teacher or a consort (ie someone who has had a DUTY life giving selfless support to a partner or function) – is likely to find themselves repeating this in their next life. Also, they will take on the mantle of this earlier and earlier in life as they develop more facility in the role, eventually becoming so adept at this that their ability becomes CONSCIOUS. This is part of the human promise but in actuality relates to the possibility of ascending to Sun level.

It is worth pointing out here that in terms of future life, REBORNS cannot escape the Planet because their chosen role belongs entirely with life as it happens here, on this planet, where conditions are UNIQUE. Having said this, the Planet is particularly interested in REBORNS because they represent the kind of REFINED CONTENT she needs to evolve into a Star. The other point worth mentioning here is that, having dedicated one's life to REBORN CONTENT it is very difficult to undo this and take up the quest for the ENTITY OF SELF again.

ELEMENTAL INVOLVEMENT: THE OTHER SIDE OF THE IDENTITY COIN

At this point the reader must grasp the fact that the Planet herself has a great entourage of unseen aides that are vital to her maintenance and evolution. Of these, **elementals** (the original maintainers of the planetary system and organic life) are most important, as is **Earth Life** (which had its origins in the elementals and now acts as a maintenance system for flora life on the planet).

Elemental content in us is important in that, on the one hand, it is vital in the building of a correct IDENTITY that matches the INNER Self and shows the person how best to cope with the elemental within. It is also the Elemental aspect of us that drives us to do – in children it pushes us to climb a tree, play football and experience the extraordinary capability of the human machine and it is obviously therefore very, very important in the reborn life, so much of which is consecrated to doing.

On the other hand, elemental involvement allows greater natural connections to other life forms. It is important that, although by and large planetary elementals shun human beings (who for them are a violent disruption of the natural world) it is possible for a human to make the right kind of signal which invites an elemental to power and assist their work of life. "Elementalising" **the Entity of Self** is very important and as a consequence, the Elemental may choose to attend the person and stay connected to them through many lifetimes.

THE LIVING EVENT OF THE HUMAN LIFE

Equally, earth life may choose to become involved with the person and to assist them in their purpose should that person be able "to dance to the rhythms of the little Earth people". It is important to realise that in all things natural there is a **need to serve** but some things can be compelled to serve in enterprises of dubious merit and other things are pristine. With regard to elemental life, the Red and the Green can be suborned into warped practice but the Blue, White and Yellow cannot.

Elementals may also choose to attend the **Reborn**, drawn to their **Content** rather than the **Entity of Self**. It would be unthinkable that persons of high promise within the planetary domain would not be accompanied and that there would not be a **great circle of higher life forms** watching over rare and important CONTENT because, as has been mentioned previously, much is riding upon the Planet's ability to manufacture higher containment that is her passport to star level.

Furthermore, the Reborn life can experience **divinatory beginnings as a pre-cursor to individual experience,** in the sense that all domains can be connected via sympathetic resonance in the way of kind goes to kind – as an example, great music or art must be linked to other great music and art and must draw things of kind to itself. Divination relies on making connection to things of the same frequency, in the same way as if you ring a particular tuning fork, say "c", all identical tuning forks will resonate in sympathy. It is entirely possible for a person to **make connection** or **divination to the Ancestry of an Art or Ability**; in exactly this way the poet and artist William Blake tried to understand and connect to the painting techniques of the artist Raphael and was so successful that he eventually said **Raphael himself turned up in his room and explained them to him**. This is very likely to be true. In this case,

the resonant vibration of Blake's content would have created a demand to which Raphael (himself based in the **Animated** worlds) would have had to respond. This is playing the **Celestial Event** (that is a higher than planetary occurrence) in an ethereal way.

THE LIVING EVENT OF THE HUMAN LIFE

DEVELOPING A PEDIGREE OR CASTE OF CONTENT (AS OPPOSED TO AN ENTITY OF SELF)

In further consideration of the situation of **Reborns**, it is important to see that people like this have a pedigree or caste of CONTENT rather than a pedigree or caste that relates to entity of Self.

Reborns may target themselves on a generality of domain – say music or art – but end up specialising in a particular area of expertise; Beethoven's life led him to music in which he was highly versatile and his specialisation led him to genius.

Furthermore, "reborns" can also be important functionaries – during World War 2, General Patton is reputed to have told a subordinate exactly where the battle would be fought, insisting that he had fought a battle at exactly that point a thousand years previously; this suggests that some reborns re-enact not only roles but occasions and events, presumably refining and **improving the content** of what they do at each step.

The greater reborns are those who specialise in the natural life rather than in a cultural proficiency; these are the lives which the Planet particularly wants to take to herself.

The great pitfall that the reborn must try to avoid is that of **autism** given that **autistic people struggle to understand this culture. Autism** can be seen as an inability to compute normal cultural behaviour, not seeming to understand what others are feeling, unable to express emotion and finding it hard to make friends or interact socially. This manifests as a **deficiency** in cultural roles and contrasts oddly with often **extraordinary mental ability**. Beethoven is a **prime example** of this, all efforts to make him behave failed and once, having pushed his way up to the Archduke, he claimed it was quite impossible for him to follow conventional codes of behaviour. The Archduke smiled and said "We will have to accept Beethoven as he is." Referring to the princes at court Beethoven remarked "There are and always will be thousands of princes but there is only one Beethoven!"

Nonetheless, it is possible for **reborns** to learn how to function smoothly within culture (perhaps by acquiring the right kind of identity?) or perhaps they require a "reboot" of added values (presumably only possible in a future life?)

Unquestionably, reborns rarely guess at what they do; like Beethoven, it is as if they are listening to a **hidden internal voice** dictating what they need to do next. The "trial and error", "hit and miss" approach to life that most of us experience is quite alien to them unless within the field of social engagement.

What we must ask ourselves is to what degree reborns ever had a real-life choice in deciding their future? Did the Inner Self actually make the decision to follow the route of the Reborn or was the decision made for them by circumstance or the family tree? Certainly, it seems likely that a "newbie" born into the Bach family would have small chance of avoiding a musical path and both Beethoven and Mozart had music thrust upon them by domineering fathers from a very early age. We will probably never know if any of these men started by chance or by **the choice event of the Inner Self**. If the choice was not by their own hand (and there must be innumerable children who have their futures predetermined by

THE LIVING EVENT OF THE HUMAN LIFE

ambitious parents) then it may be that the life of a reborn is temporary and may in the future be overtaken by the person's **life event**.

Whether the choice of path is by their own hand or not, **the path of the out-front practitioner or performer is unquestionably a lonely one**; returning to Beethoven, his personal life was difficult, isolated and he was clearly much misunderstood even by those one would expect to be sympathetic (apparently one of his early teachers remarked of him "as a composer, he is hopeless.").

Finally, there are **specific personal requirements** that belong with the Reborn path. Clearly, to have selected this way (or had it selected for one by someone or something else) means that the person has stepped away from the quest for the **Entity of Self** and taken a different direction. By pursuing another kind of life and dedicating themselves to it, they forfeit the original Creational promise of self-fulfilment.

Furthermore, as reborns often pursue their chosen path with fierce singularity and purpose they will find it very difficult to recover **the original human quest for self-emancipation**. It may be that the Beethovens, Mozarts and other reborn genius find their choice of path ultimately fulfils their lust for learning and the desire for passion. However, alongside people like these one must put the huge numbers of reborns who have coalesced around a profession or path which is wholly cultural and is likely to only offer an eternal repetition of the fact of themselves. The Planet is extremely interested in the **content** of a Beethoven or a Mozart because it helps her to build her stellar core so, although people like this forgo the fulfilment of the Entity of Self they still have the possibility of ascension.

Chapter 7:
2nd Afterlife Settings
(Stage 7)

THE CONSIDERATIONS OF 2ND AFTER- LIFE SETTINGS

In which we consider the after-life stage prior to the third physical life; the considerations of Reincarnation; Transformation (where change itself changes the rules); further considerations of Reborn; Activity outside of settings.

THE LIVING EVENT OF THE HUMAN LIFE

THE CONSIDERATIONS OF REINCARNATION

It is at this point that, having experienced two physical lives, the second of which is a replay of the former, we arrive at the starting place for Reincarnation. This represents a new investiture for the Entity of Self, in which the WHAT of the two previous lives is repeated and will hopefully result in a refinement of content and attendance that is a passport to either further lives or an ascensional future beyond planetary.

In this scenario, the person will retain some Awoken or Conscious content from previous lives and will also be in a position to repeat the habitual self in roles experienced previously in that these may well already be deeply engraved upon the person. Remember, the What may have crystallised around a life of great suffering and difficulty; the life of say, a medieval peasant would have been extremely harsh and probably very singular in its address to living, this is as likely to have survived death as someone who spent their time dedicated to say, being a nun or monk.

At this moment, the person may have developed AWARENESS as part of their developing planetary being and as a feature of their habitual life; they may also have a welded memory of previous experience or lives that they are able to carry forward into their next physical existence. This is rather like the genetic memory that some dogs carry from their forebears; those that come from generations of dogs that have worked sheep, or been service or gun dogs hardly require any training in these disciplines because they have an innate ability in them that just requires "bringing out".

Equally, some transient lines seem to carry an indelible print in that people may remark of a child 'oh he's definitely a Brown' referring to much more than just a physical resemblance – on the other hand, they might shake their heads and wonder about a child who appears to be a 'changeling' and nothing like them at all!

Alongside all this, the memory of physical trauma or defect may also be carried forward; it is surprising how many reincarnation stories which carry a sense of actuality and realism about them start from a vivid and frightening memory of a violent ending to a previous life. There is also fascinating evidence for a co-relation between birth marks and defects in Dr Ian Stevenson's excellent book "Where Reincarnation and Biology Intersect"[1] in which he cites about ninety cases where there is a correspondence between the "birth marks on the child and similar marks or distinguishing features present on the body of the reincarnated personality during their lifetime such as wounds, injuries and other stigmata". Stevenson also refers to cases where "experimental" birthmarks were made on the dead and dying, including twenty cases from Thailand and Myanmar (Burma)in the hope that it would be easy to identify that person if they reincarnate; in eighteen out of twenty cases the previous person was later identified by the mark. It is also interesting to note that in the vast majority of these cases the reincarnated person turns up again in the family line (or transient tree).

Obviously, it is to be expected that there would be more openness and cognisance about these matters in the Far East where reincarnation is often an article of faith. (These writings are

---

[1] "Where Reincarnation and Biology Intersect" Ian Stevenson MD Greenwood Publishing Group 1997 ISBN 0-275-95189-8

THE LIVING EVENT OF THE HUMAN LIFE

intended to help people find the real truth and what ACTUALITY is; if a person cannot see beyond their religion, cultural education or ideology, it may not help them).

In addition, it is interesting that in Dr Stevenson's[2] excellent book, a high proportion of the cases he cites in the Far East in which his evidence seems irrefutable, were instances in which the young child remembered a life as a blood relative. This suggests that at least in these parts of the world reincarnation via the family tree or transient line is extremely common.

It is also important to note that there is a large degree of what can only be described as "pot luck" in the circumstances the reincarnating finds themselves being born; Dr Stevenson cites twenty-four cases of Burmese children who remembered a previous life as a Japanese soldier killed in Burma in World War 2. Many of these children "had traits that are unusual in Burmese families but characteristic of Japanese persons, especially Japanese soldiers" (Page 197: Children who Remember Previous Lives"). This suggests that after dying the disembodied person may have a tendency to hang around the location in which they died rather than return to their place of origin and much of Dr Stevenson's research seems to bear this out. It is a curious thought but how many German soldiers who died in the fields of France actually ended up reincarnating as a French person! However, to continue with the main theme if this chapter, it is clear that for the most part, the person awaiting reincarnation is looking for another opportunity to "pick- up" the story of their life, although this won't be without cost as there may

---

[2] There are a number of references in this chapter to Ian Pretyman Stevenson (October 31, 1918 – February 8, 2007) Children Who Remember Previous Lives: A Question of Reincarnation: McFarland & Co 31 March. 2001 ISBN 978-0786409136

well be aspects of themselves that need refinement or even erasure in order to continue and this may invoke much suffering and difficulty in the future and be a prime factor in their choice of physical life or role.

As a consequence of wrong or unfortunate manufacture in a past life, some structures in the person may need to be broken down, some may need building, and the life will be looking for opportunities that allow this to happen. There will be a search for suitable roles and stories that allow the person to accrue the right kind of experience to change their particular script and help them on their journey towards their real Self. Also, there will be some future physical lives that carry a particular power and charisma which would be highly sought after; as an example, EVENT lives are like the bubbles in the boiling pot of experience – these are lives which facilitate important points in human history, a prime example of which is Winston Churchill, who came here to do an important job. Many of the most famous lives in history (and probably many anonymous ones) were EVENT lives who needed to do something to try to keep the human race on the right track. It is tempting to consider certain scientists, as an example, whose lives transformed the health and well-being of literally billions of people as EVENT lives that came here to do a job or initiate something. (Louis Pasteur for example, who pioneered microbiological technique and developed pasteurisation, thus radically altering life for countless people. Another example is Florence Nightingale, whose legacy of wound hygiene saved millions of lives). Event lives (which are clearly also duty or service lives) are likely to recur whenever there is a need and one is tempted to conclude that transient trees have their own Event lives, waiting in the wings until they are needed.

THE CONSIDERATIONS OF TRANSFORMATION

The dictionary defines transformation as a change of form or function and suggests that the person is looking for opportunities in their next life that will allow them to take an entirely new direction in self. This may include breaking away from a transient tree (sometimes apparent when a child appears to be almost a "changeling", so different are they from their siblings), changing gender or choosing to seek out influences and identification that will facilitate change.

It is feasible for the unborn person to seek out a life where change itself changes the rules; as an example, a person might seek out a DUTY life in which surrender to a higher Purpose dramatically changes the WHAT of them, or they might try to find a life of suffering that undoes unfortunate things in themselves. In this situation, the difficulties a person experiences can re-programme them back to a correct course and re-awaken the Entity of Self in them.

Clearly, in the next physical life, whatever the person identifies with and allows to influence them is going to have radical effects on their ongoing possibility of life. There is also, obviously, the fact that decisions made in the Afterlife before conception will not be remembered, as hardly anyone seems to reincarnate with a total recall of a former existence even though some may get tantalising glimpses of previous lives.

Certainly, the likelihood is that even those with vivid recall of a

SECOND AFTERLIFE SETTINGS

different life when they are young will have lost it by about six, as a consequence of engaging with the pressing needs of their new life. People may even have to change gender if that is the best option available, which perhaps accounts for people who feel uncomfortable in themselves because they are a different sex this time around. There are many reincarnation stories that bear this out: in "Children who Remember Previous Lives", Chapter 4, Ian Stevenson cites the case of Ma Tin Aung Mayo, who was born on December 26th 1953 in the village of Nathul in Upper Burma. Whilst pregnant the little girl's mother, Daw Aye Tin dreamt on three occasions that she was being followed by a stocky Japanese soldier who said he was coming to live with her and her husband. When she was older, the little girl had a phobia for airplanes and later claimed that she had been a Japanese cook stationed at Nahul during World War 2 and that she had been killed when an allied plane had strafed the village. She talked about having had a wife and family in Japan and at about four, when found crying for no apparent reason said she missed Japan. Ma Tin's most remarkable behaviour was" her extreme boyishness. She insisted on dressing in men's clothes and wearing her hair in a boy's style. This eventually led to a crisis at her school when the authorities insisted she come to school dressed appropriately as a girl. She refused; they were adamant so she dropped out of school at about eleven." Throughout her life Ma Tin Aung Mayo remained "strongly masculine in her sexual orientation...she had "no interest in marrying a man. On the contrary she said she would like to have a wife. She obviously thought of herself as a man and disliked being considered a woman." There are other reincarnation stories that bear out the idea of "gender jumping" but the story of Ma Tin Aung Mayo is one of the most well-documented and convincing. (For further details see Pages 60 -62 "Children Who Remember Previous Lives"). It is also interesting to note that by majority, those who clearly remembered being the opposite sex previously had settled to their new gender after they had been through puberty.

Alongside gender-jumping, it is equally possible for an animal to "species leap" into human form, if they have managed to gather human content previously, especially if they had lived previously in close proximity to humans. It is likely that domestic animals such as dogs, cats and birds are the choice candidates for "species leap" as living alongside human beings would give them the opportunity to gather the necessary CONTENT; there would hardly be much opportunity for this if one were a wildebeest in the Serengeti! It is obviously difficult if not impossible to find people who truly remember a previous life as say, a cat. On the other hand, there are many instances of domestic animals (often in rescue centres) that appear to display nurturing behaviour indiscriminately to other species than their own. This suggests that they are motivated by something outside the dynamic of their particular kind; however, it is appreciated that this can never be more than a hypothesis.

As a consequence of the aeons of time in which history has been happening on the Planet and its aggregation (not to mention the twists and turns history has taken over the millennia, many very regrettable) we now have a fossilised Culture which is no longer in harmony with the purposes of either the Planet or Creation itself. This has resulted in dynamics and ability in people and the culture that are really offset to natural purpose and which carry new forms of expression and roles that the life may gravitate towards. Examples of these would include the vast number of different economic or social roles – from engine driver to mechanic to airline pilot to professional football or tennis player, to name just a few- that have been generated by the Industrial Revolution. Because of these unique circumstances (which probably don't exist anywhere else in

Creation,) it is possible for a person's CONTENT to accrue around such roles, the upshot of which would be the need to find a similar outplay for their life in the future. Again, this possibility offers no possibility of progression beyond the Planet and, as with "Reborns" would represent a path that is virtually impossible to escape. Alongside this, it is impossible to underestimate the unseen effect of the remnants of antiquity culture. As mentioned previously, the planetary age and the number of cultures that the human race has lived through is vastly greater than today's historians are prepared to give credence to. This is not just an academic consideration, because there is a record of everything that has happened here stored in the Planet's Astral, Ethereal and Animated domains which has impacted on all subsequent cultures up until and including today's. Much of this has already helped mould the story of the human race and continues to do so today. Ancient Egypt particularly seems very keen to exert its influence on today's culture and people and is perhaps behind the mesmerising effect that exhibitions such as that of Tutankhamun has upon people.

Whilst awaiting the opportunity of a new physical life, the person must be to a degree be aware of their domains of possibility the limitations imposed on them by their embedded content. They must also be cognisant of the fact that they have a "sell-by date" in that the time they have available is fixed by the quality and durability of their content (though the Afterlife Road trip may last for many thousands of years – it depends what you're made of!) In a sense, the reincarnated content could be "hedging its bets" and possibly acting in a way that will prevent total loss or failure if things do not go well in the next life – after all, there are no guarantees in the roller-coaster ride of culture and life on this Planet as it happens today.

THE LIVING EVENT OF THE HUMAN LIFE

The person may be heading into a series of "rise and fall" lives in which they struggle to maintain a content which will allow some sort of continuance.

CONSIDERATIONS OF REBORN (REBORN CONTINUES)

It must be noted that even if the previous physical life resulted in a life of CONTENT rather than an emancipation of the Entity of Self (the genuine person) there remain options available which would allow the life to re-naturalise back to their origins; it is going to depend very much on what is available in the "in- between" state of the after- life and what the person can stretch to. However, obviously the driving forces of a previous life are still operating kinetically and are likely to push the unborn person in a specific direction that results from previous contents and inclinations. Equally, there may be insistent pressure from the person's transient tree which compels them to continue to pursue the reborn line- it is impossible to overestimate the power and influence a person's planetary tree exerts upon them.

It is important to understand that everything that has happened on the Planet remains stored in the astral and ethereal domains and constitutes a powerful occult content that the knowledgeable person can connect to, have a dialogue with and even re-enact themselves; this has to do with the practice of mumming which in ancient times meant linking to the energies of a previous and significant point in history (say the passion of Jesus Christ) and allowing that event to be played out through the people present. Clearly, the participants would have to be of high quality personally and also able to keep themselves "out of the way" in order to allow something or someone else to use them as a living theatre.

In the same way, the person with reborn content is able to link directly to previous personal history and carry it forward into a future life. It may even begin to crystallise into a new identity, not based on the original Creational and planetary input but on the content the person accumulated in their previous physical life. Eventually, this may even allow the person to move away from being a Reborn back into the realms of reincarnation; equally the acquisition of sufficient content can allow someone to make the journey from Reincarnation to Reborn. Very little is set in stone here.

By and large, however, Reborns have crystallised around a specific content and will be seeking a suitable "host" in the shape of a role or family line to facilitate the growth of that content. In their reincarnation, this may result in the early onset of "mild genius" as the life coalesces around a previous content and virtually "picks up" from where they were before. Equally, the person may exhibit autistic symptoms in that reborns have no identity carried forward from previous lives and may therefore find it hard to understand emotions or social situations where others are at ease. An easy-to-understand example of this is the character Raymond played by Dustin Hoffman in the celebrated film Rain Man.

Generally, in reborns, having awakened without human identity, Content and Embodiment replace the Self. In their next physical life, they will naturally be drawn to opportunities for greater development within their chosen specialisation; the opportunity to excel in their chosen field and become a maestro is obviously paramount. It is likely that, within the sphere of Afterlife Connection, there are "embassies" that help channel people with specific reborn inclinations into the right kind of life. Although born without identity, the more a person engraves the content of something else upon themselves the more skilled they become in it and with time the Persona or role and the Psyche or mind of the reborn becomes ACTUAL. It is also possible for the person to import a new entity of self, based entirely upon the new content and even able to activate higher brain function of a divinatory nature.

It may be that the Planet, whose greater intention is to gather fine content that will facilitate her evolution to star level, has more interest in Reborns of the right calibre than anything else. Essentially, these are the planetary players par excellence who will stay-at-home, finessing what they do until the Planet takes them to her Ethereal heart until they are needed in the future. Reborns may also encompass duty lives who are in service to the Planet and the Human Race; these are more likely to form up around the right content rather than seek out the right identity, though clearly, they also need the right role and period of history to be of optimum use.

THE LIVING EVENT OF THE HUMAN LIFE

ACTIVITY OUTSIDE OF SETTINGS – THE PLANETARY 'LEAP' PROCESS

Note beforehand; all activity outside of settings can only happen with the full compliance of the Chromos that regulates planetary events and conditions here (The Chromos can be likened to the external membrane of a cell within the body that regulates the homeostatic condition within the cell).

To return to the pre third life settings generally, there are other features to consider here. Humans naturally tend to look at things exclusively from the human standpoint and are largely only hazily aware of the other life forms with which we share the Planet, particularly those that inhabit the unseen worlds all around us. These include that of Elementals, which existed here long before life generally had crystallised into physical form and which even today play an unseen but vital part in the Planet's Maintenance systems. It has already been mentioned that humans are elemental themselves and it is this part of them that drives the child to walk, to climb a tree, to run a race and to generally make full use of the marvellous opportunity of the human design and faculty. It is important to remember that humans have an inner life (known as BEING) and an outer life (ELEMENTAL) and that it is essential that a person maintains both, otherwise they rob themselves of the opportunity to grow.

It is no doubt difficult for the modern mind to conceive of an unseen form of life with a particular interest in specific human lives, but nonetheless it is so. As an example, there are healing elementals

SECOND AFTERLIFE SETTINGS

which can and do operate through human beings; often the human being themselves have no idea that this is the source of their ability to heal, they believe that it is them personally that has "the healing touch" whereas the truth is they are simply the local "post office" for the ability. There are children who have the innate ability to heal which can only have been carried through from a previous life and the supposition has to be that a healing elemental remained connected to them almost as part of an entourage in their afterlife.

Healing elementals are just one aspect of this; the elemental worlds are a powerhouse regime for certain aspects of human life and have associated with certain kinds of human activity for millennia (the Druids, as an example, used certain types of Elementals in their rituals) and it is likely that a life that has previously associated with these entities will carry through the connection into their afterlife and beyond. Subsequently, this connection is highly likely to influence the pregnant mother and will predispose her towards particular moods, feelings and inclinations. There has been a long history on this Planet in which human beings and human organisations (including the Church) have harnessed the power of the Elementals for their own purposes, sometimes benign, sometimes not so good. It is worth reflecting here that some Elemental life form can be used in a deviant practice but some most assuredly cannot.

All planetary domain life form is controlled by the Chromos which acts like the membrane of a cell and regulates what can happen within the cell. This includes the regulation of form both in its origins and in its current outplay. Everything on the Planet must abide by planetary law (as laid down by the Chromos), including planetary form containment that might choose to attend the reincarnating person. This is true throughout Creation – wherever

THE LIVING EVENT OF THE HUMAN LIFE

life goes it must have a suitable containment and abide by local criteria, laws and protocols. An extreme example of this (but it makes the point) is noted by Robert Temple in "the Sirius Mystery"[3] when he says that were we to visit Sirius B, a white dwarf, "we would not even be a fraction of an inch high. We would be flat, pulled in by the gravity."

Therefore, even though there may be a coming and going between the astral, ethereal and even the animated horizons of higher life occurring, it must all be authorised and mandated by the Chromos.

Nonetheless, it is possible for a developing life to borrow and lend back CONTENT from higher realms but the understanding is that the person makes themselves upon the content, they cannot keep it. This is essentially something the Planet has done in that she has "borrowed" Sun level content to assist her in her development – this is self-evident in that the Pentagram is a Sun level structure and the human is itself pentagrammic. This is rather like borrowing money from the bank to start a business; eventually the proprietor can keep the profit but he still needs to pay the original loan to the Bank.

Above and beyond these considerations, the person awaiting rebirth may be seeking a special role that create different future options for their life. The life may even experience a calling that draws them to a duty of life within the planetary domains. This may include being offered the opportunity to take on a particular role if they are deemed suitable; there clearly are watchers and observers

---

[3] Robert Temple : The Sirius Mystery. Arrow 1999 ISBN 0 09 925744 0 Page 81

from different domains, from beyond the physical that keep an eye on planetary affairs and try to steer events in the right direction. These would function rather like the "head-hunters" of the modern business world that seek out promising young people in order to offer them a job. Clearly, this would involve the creation of special roles – leaders, diviners, teachers that are able to actualise planetary plans - even universal policemen (the function of whom would have to be to ensure things stay within acceptable parameters here on the Planet – they would clearly have to be "unbreakable" in their allegiance to creational purpose). Strange as this might sound to the twenty-first century mind, it is unthinkable that the higher realms of an intelligent Creation would not maintain an embassy on its furthest outpost that kept a watchful eye on events there.

Chapter 8: (Stage 8) Third Physical Life

The third physical life (possibly the first of many repetitional lives); the considerations of the Continuous Revolution; new Difficulty of Self – unsettlement of the Inner Life; Entity Identity, Elemental and Earth Life; the considerations of the Way of the New Genius (Mental Inner Life Development and Self- Maintenance); the considerations of Greater Order and Criteria.

THE CONSIDERATIONS OF THE CONTINUOUS REVOLUTION OF MANY LIVES

In this scenario, the person enters a series of repetitional Life or Lives which ideally will lead to a continuous refinement of their CORE CONTENT and the start of a greater planetary event with greatly improved natural connections. Ideally, the life is now more on track with WHAT it was intended to be, rather than sidetracked into a cultural event which is the upshot of thousands of years of wrong manufacture on the Planet.

Rather than just being subject to the vicissitudes and vagaries of the culture into which they are born, people may now have the advantage of a purposeful choice of Self-View, and the word "purpose" is very important here. Mostly, people tend to think that they themselves are in charge of their lives and that they make their own decisions about the direction their lives take, but unfortunately this is rarely the case – on the contrary, virtually everything that happens to people is down to happenstance and the roulette wheel of life. There are obviously a fortunate few who are exceptionally lucky, or rich, or both, that are able to be self-determined with regard to their life and the old adage that "people stand aside for a person who knows what they want" is certainly very true; however, it is likely that the choices they make are based on the need for cultural prowess or family happiness (not that these are unimportant) rather than the need to develop their CORE self. This very much depends upon a person deliberately deciding WHAT they want to be in say, ten years' time, hopefully measured against ACTUALITY and REALITY rather than a personal whim, and setting themselves a series of short and long-term goals that will lead to this. It is certainly true that if a person is unhappy with their life now it is certain that unless they make a firm decision about change of direction, and deliberately implement it their situation in ten years' time will be the same, if not worse.

This might include efforts to end undefined or unseen habitual practices by overlaying them with more productive and beneficial ways that take the person closer to their next development step in terms of living. Generally, people are entirely unconscious of the habitual ways that govern their lives- how many times can you not remember whether you have locked your front door because you have done it unconsciously, just a tiny example of how we are all ruled by habit. Anyone who has ever tried to give up smoking or lose weight knows how hard it is to overcome the tyranny of habit. For this reason, people find themselves trapped in attitudes and mind sets that are extremely personally costly. However, as a person begins to develop a clearer Self View based upon real things, it becomes easier to take control and steer one's life in a different direction. It really is the difference between allowing oneself to be washed hither and thither on the river of life, or making the decision to be in charge of the vessel of SELF.

It is very important here not to be caught by cultural notions of "right" and "wrong", given that these are very temporary and local in practise; what is thought highly moral and desirable in one culture can be utterly despised in another – in the West burping after a meal is considered rude, whereas in China it is thought of as a compliment to the chef!

In place of "right" and "wrong", a person needs to ask whether something is useful or not useful to the Purpose they are pursuing;

something that adds to their CORE self is obviously beneficial, something that takes away is not. Unfortunately, as there are no guarantees for life on the Planet, the reincarnating person is likely to experience a ride of success or failure, of sometimes doing well and sometimes falling back. There are no certainties or guarantees at this level of Creation; the life can still fail here, or fall back and need another life to recover lost ground.

Nonetheless, there are opportunities to develop greater intuition (from the Being life), greater initiative (from the Elemental outplay) and greater cognisance (from higher mental faculties), since hopefully some of these qualities have already been somewhat seeded in previous physical lifetimes. Equally, a person who is on an ascending path in themselves may already have a platform of discipline founded on understanding what is reasonable and advantageous to their real life. They may also be driven by hidden fears and disenchantment with what their lives have accomplished so far. Just as a "newbie" has a freshness and innocence about them, there is probably a grain of truth in the notion of an "old soul", which is a cliché used to describe someone who seems to have a wisdom and maturity beyond their years.

It is at this point in a person's journey, assuming that the overall trend of their lives is upward, they begin to experience a Greater Awakening of the Inner Self (which may be regarded as a Second Conception) They are likely to find what is culturally available unsatisfactory, repetitive, even robotic, because generally culture offers roles and distraction rather than the fulfilment of the promise of self.

As the Inner Self awakens, the person's **Prescence and Persona** (the Elemental expression of the Entity of Self) begins to grow. This

THE LIVING EVENT OF THE HUMAN LIFE

gradually superimposes the roles of life, which can be thought of as the masks a person needs to "get by" in cultural life. Examples of this are manifold, one only has to think of the behaviour that is required in the workplace, in a shopping centre, when visiting family or friends to name but a few. Truly, Shakespeare was inspired when he wrote "All the world's a stage and all the men and women merely players" (As You Like It Act 2 Scene 7)!

It is not within the scope of this book to make a detailed study of Presence and Persona (though future publications may include this) but suffice it to say these constitute a natural expression for the Entity of Self that include many arts and abilities that are currently lost to the Human (even though they are in fact just dormant and need the right kind of Work to awaken them). Today, people of this calibre are rare; if you were to meet one the word "charismatic" would immediately spring to mind. This would be to do with their radiation (in that their CONTENT would be exceptionally bright and refined) rather than having to do with the illusory world of celebrity culture.

The more the person "wakes up" to the actuality of Life and the proposition of being true to their inner core, the more they surrender their old self to a new Vision of Self. This must be accompanied by the right kind of Work or the person will simply "fall back to sleep" and return to the comfortability of roles and living as part of a cultural collective. This is always a danger because unfortunately we do not live in a culture that promotes the Entity of Self; there have been very advanced cultures in antiquity that have been entirely focused on the fulfilment of planetary purpose and the emancipation of the individual CORE but the world today is not organised in that way and in any case, we have a difficult and deviant history to contend with.

THE NEW DIFFICULTY OF SELF-UNSETTLEMENT OF THE INNER LIFE

Having awoken to the need to develop the Entity of Self, the person faces a difficult and challenging journey. As they live in a world that is geared up to entirely different goals and importances, the reincarnating person is likely to feel entirely at odds with everything around them. Their Inner Life will experience unsettlement and it will be obvious that change is essential if they are going to meet the requirements of their new Vision of Self by surrendering the Old Self. It is self-evident that the ways that belong to the cultural self will only produce more of the same and the person is going to have to develop different attitudes and ways if they are to meet the requirements of the new developing CORE. Struggle and Difficulty will become the order of the day if the person is going to engage in the originating of a new or forming core. Generally, as a species humans cherish comfortability, but by this stage the person is likely to be driven by a general dissatisfaction with themselves and what is currently available.

There are also difficulties in the shape of those who do not want their friends and relatives to change. A person's transient line has invested a great deal of time and energy into moulding them in a particular shape and they are likely to be unhappy at what they see to be personality changes. A lot of family life revolves around fixed roles and people feel uncomfortable and ill at ease if those roles start to slip; almost everyone has experienced the awkwardness of finding themselves in an unfamiliar situation where they have no idea what to say or how to behave – it simply means the person has no suitable role in themselves available.

THE LIVING EVENT OF THE HUMAN LIFE

Equally, virtually everyone has had a cultural formal education which is very useful in terms of earning a living and making one's way in the world, but which is mostly useless when it comes to developing the Entity of Self. For this a person needs to make a profound and detailed study of the Natural Laws (which govern the Planet and the Solar System and the Creation in which we live) as well as what it means to be human (looking at the human as the highest form of life on a planet which contains a myriad of different life forms). It is highly likely that there will be conflict in the person between their previous formal education and the new knowledge they need to acquire for a development journey.

In addition, the person may carry not only the wrong manufacture of a previous life but also unfortunate psychologies, beliefs and attitudes generated by their current history. The saying "Ignorance is bliss" is very true, because the more a person wakes up to the actuality of their situation, the more they perceive the need to change or to adopt better views (even if they are only temporary views that get them a little further up the road).

Throughout history, there have always been people who, unhappy with what is generally available in life, have chosen to pursue the less well-trodden esoteric paths laid down by those who have gone before; some of these people have been anonymous, some are a source of fascination and wonder even today and some have been relegated to the realms of myth and mystery. They include such names as Lao T'se (the supposed author of the Tao), the legendary Yellow Emperor (also Tao), the famous architect, doctor and sage Imhotep, Ralph Waldo Emerson, Leonardo da Vinci, Elizabeth 1's astrologer Dr Dee, to name but a few. Some have worked alone; many have been the interface between the culture and an esoteric group. All of them have endeavoured to follow a path based on Actuality and Natural Law rather than the temporary truths of their particular culture and time.

Of these, one of the most celebrated was the figure of Hermes Trismegistus, who was reputedly part of the Hermetic Tradition and to whom is attributed the famous paraphrase "As above so below". This refers to Natural and Creational Law and simply says that the human, the Planet and our local Solar System all work according to the same laws as the higher echelons of Creation (although esoteric wisdom tells us that we, on the Planet, live a long way from Creation in its finest form and are subject to more laws than say, constellational level). Therefore, the way of wisdom and enlightenment is to build one's life on understandings founded on natural law and process, which have a permanency that transitory human affairs lack.

It is not possible to do more than touch on these Laws in this book, but suffice it to say that ultimately, they are very profound and very simple; it stands to reason that if Creation worked on rules like those that govern human attitudes and behaviour the whole affair would have come to an end long ago!

It is imperative that a person wishing to develop their Entity of Self undertakes a deep study of these laws; such a study allows people to determine what is REAL and ACTUAL for themselves, rather than having to take another person's teaching on trust or submit to the vagaries of faith and belief. Also, as Life originally issued from Creation (the Spawning), a person needs to build the Entity of Self and their new Life upon the laws that govern Creation rather than personal whim – to put it bluntly, if you want to be a successful football player you have to follow the rules of the game, if you want to play Creation's game you must do likewise! Otherwise, ultimately, you will have no game to play; we are granted a degree of licence here because we live on the outskirts of Creation that is simply not available nearer to Creation's core.

However, to continue with the journey of the reincarnated life that has chosen to develop their inner self, given that they have made this decision they will inevitably face inner struggles alongside the struggles born from living in the culture itself. Having grown up in a world which is geared to the demands of modern life rather than self-emancipation, and having inherited the deviant works of History and Culture, it is clear that no development journey based on real things is going to be easy. The reincarnating life has to gradually chase out the lower aspects of themselves and replace them with higher views and higher abilities.

In cultural life, people surround themselves with roles that facilitate the life they lead and eventually, this constitutes an IDENTITY. This is necessary if a person is to survive in culture but it is in no way suitable as a containment for the ACTUALITY of SELF.

ENTITY IDENTITY, THE ELEMENTAL AND EARTH LIFE

In order to build the right kind of embodiments for the genuine SELF, a person needs to undertake a deep study of the Unseen worlds that surround our planet and which are all around us. Learning to sense, see and feel the unseen and to develop abilities like seeing electrically, sensing auras and divining knowledge is a vital part of reclaiming our lost human heritage. Being divinatory, being clairvoyant, making connection to life forms like the Elementals, Healing forces and Earth Life (so-called fairies, elves, gnomes, sylphs and so forth) are all part of the human inheritance long abandoned by the human race in favour of technology.(This is not to point the finger of blame because it is appreciated that today's humans have inherited rather than instigated the accumulated problems of history) No doubt many will scoff at the idea of Earth life and its ilk but one has to wonder where the images, stories and folklore of such things have actually come from? There is virtually no culture on earth with roots in antiquity that does not have its own unique stories about these life forms. In the time-honoured classic, "The Boy Who Saw True"[1], a young boy of the late Victorian period wrote a diary in which he described the electro-magnetic realms he saw and the Earth life he noticed, not realising for a long time that what was obvious to him was entirely invisible to other people. In the book he describes "a funny old gnome who lives inside s "lovely old tree "in his uncle's garden who has "great long thin legs and wears a red cap though the rest of him is like the colour of a tree". He adds "sometimes he comes out of his tree and goes prancing about in the grass" (This is likely to be a wood elf rather than a gnome as gnomes are not connected to trees.).

The Fairy Feller's Master-Stroke
Dadd painted 1855 -1864

The young boy also describes visiting Keswick and

---

[1] The Boy Who Saw True "The time-honoured classic of the Paranormal" Rider Books 2005 ISBN 9781844131501

seeing "lovely clouds with beautiful fairies in them who "made the clouds into all sorts of funny shapes like castles and some of the clouds they made into things like huge funny looking animals" (rather than fairies these are clearly sylphs which are connected to the air aspects of the Planet). He also mentions going to Birkdale (a seaside resort) "to watch the fairies playing among the stones and seaweed on the seashore" and much more. The Irish poet W B Yeats (who obviously believed that Earth life actually existed) wrote the famous "Fairy and Folk Tales of The Irish Peasantry"[2] which is presented not as a work of fiction but as an account of the real-life experiences of the people of rural Ireland. In the seer and clairvoyant Geoffrey Hodson's charming book "Fairies at Work and Play"[3], he describes in detail many different types of Earth life as well as visions of previous cultures that obviously derive from antiquity and the akashic records (his description of a vision experienced at the Druid's Circle, a stone circle near Keswick is of particular interest).

Many poets and artists have clearly had connections to Earth life, and these connections are either implicitly or explicitly expressed in their work; the visionary poet William Blake described seeing a tree "shimmering" with what "looks like angels" (probably elf life and an elemental) and the artist Richard Dadd painted exquisite highly detailed pictures of earth life and the supernatural, which are obviously based on what he actually saw. It is important to realise that these beings are not just the source of romantic stories; they are part of the functional entourage of the planet and have a practical part to play in her development and evolution.

---

[2] Fairy and Folk Tales Of the Irish Peasantry" Edited William Butler Yeats Dover Publications New York 1991 ISBN 0-486-26941-8

[3] Geoffrey Hodson "Fairies at Work and Play" Quest Books 1982 ISBN10: 0835605531

Building an identity founded on real things is an essential part of the development of the Entity of Self and includes the initiation of restoring the Elemental life of Self. The reader will recall that the original CORE of self was partially ELEMENTAL and it is vital that the person begins to build the right kind of Elemental outplay in themselves, which would include developing abilities like connecting to the unseen worlds, becoming divinatory, becoming highly sensitive, starting to switch on higher mental faculties and much more. Having an IDENTITY that gives the right order of expression to the BEING life is essential because these two need to work in harmony together. All this adds up to a person changing and developing new skills and most of all, starting to take control of their Life and take it in the direction of their choice. Obviously, regaining Personal Control is not without cost and inevitably a person will face struggle and difficulty on the way, but this represents the deepening of a greater work on the core of SELF which holds a promise for the future. Equally, the person can hold their head up in the certain knowledge that they have, by their own hand, made definite commitments to self by their own choice and not at the hands of other people.

THE CONSIDERATIONS OF THE WAY OF THE NEW GENIUS; MENTAL INNER LIFE DEVELOPMENT AND SELF-MAINTENANCE

The first step on the pathway to emancipation of self begins when a person AWAKENS and starts to appreciate the difficulties of their own situation. At this particular time, all organic life on the planet is AWAKE in the sense that it knows what it is and the function it exists to perform; only the HUMAN is asleep and offset to its true purpose -this is the esoteric meaning behind fairy tales such as the story of the Sleeping Beauty, who awaits a silver kiss to wake her up (many esoteric truths are actually tucked away in the guise of children's stories and are, in a sense, hidden in plain sight).

The first step on the journey begins with AWAKENING, though one may have to go through a series of awakenings because staying awake is not a "given", it is very easy to fall asleep again. It is a lot easier to stay AWAKE if one has companions who are undertaking the same journey as everyone can act as a barometer for each other's state of mind.

Having AWAKENED, the next step is to begin to occupy and develop the Mental inner life of oneself which in a development sense really means "taking over an empty space".

At this point, the person needs to adapt and re-think their own ideology and mentality, altering their own mental stance and starting to add new Belief to their Works of Life. It is also very important that they learn to not take things personally if they face difficulty or criticism from others or even themselves (sometimes we are the first to bring ourselves down with automatic negative thought processes); given the state of the world we live in, the emancipation of self was never going to be a joy ride! In a way, by setting one's feet on this path we are like the salmon who have to swim against the tide to reach our destination and fulfil our purpose.

Having made the decision to be oneself, to build a life with a higher future (rather than simply suffering the ups and downs of a life struggling to survive and scrape together the necessary points to make it into another reincarnation) one has to MAINTAIN one's new SELF. This demands a continuity of practice as nothing here happens automatically, one needs definite DISCIPLINES and WAYS to maintain the new person. Like the dedicated dancer, musician or athlete, a person has to be working every day to maintain and hopefully improve their skills and understandings. Everything has to maintained here and, in the beginning, it is easier to let standards fall rather than improve them because one is working against long-standing habits in oneself that stand in opposition to new aims and purpose. It is also very important to go out on a regular basis to prove the work and one's results; this is why it is paramount that a person cross checks everything they do against the infallibility of natural and planetary law. The pursuit of the actuality of Self is not something that a person does as a hobby, it means working on the Actualities of personal domains and going out on a regular basis to prove the work and results. However, it is important that the reader grasps that this is not a chore but becomes a source of personal uplift, joy and self-confirmation.

The more a person works on the Entity of Self the more it grows and deepens and the more the person touches new things in

THE LIVING EVENT OF THE HUMAN LIFE

themselves. Higher life activities begin to occur and the person starts to connect to special entities that live in the unseen worlds but normally do not associate with humans. This further fuels the need in a person to oppose the Lower aspects of themselves (such as anger, hypocrisy, criticism and judgement) for the sake of the Higher which they, having put their feet on this path, have chosen to champion. All this starts to add a greater Content to the SELF which comes from a higher than planetary source, which allows the person to build embodiments in themselves which stretch beyond planetary level.

THE CONSIDERATIONS OF THE GREATER ORDER AND CRITERIA: THE BIGGER PICTURE THE SELF IS AIMING AT

A person needs to understand that as long as they live on the planet, they will experience the Contest for the Entity of Self and even after they have created superior embodiments in themselves and are attended by entities above planetary level, they will still be fighting a "rear guard "action against the culture and the historical traces it has left in them. Truly, we are facing an "all-out game of thrones" here (Game of Thrones being a series in which everything is cut and dried, you either win or you die).

However, as time goes on the awakened person (now well-established and fixed in purpose) develops greater refinement of Domains and starts to establish Sovereignty over Culture. As long as someone lives on the planet and has to survive in the culture, they have to surrender a certain percentage of themselves to cultural life. Obviously, the greater the percentage of time and commitment given to culture the less a person can give to the development and growth of the Entity of Self and, as they say in Hollywood, its all about the percentages!

The battle for possession of the whole SELF also includes the struggle against the resident IDENTITY, which is likely to have congealed around the person's roles (the regime of masks people have to wear in order to survive in culture) rather than the person's CORE. For this reason, they need to be very vigilant about their own internal and external processes, on a daily basis, with a view to not only liberating their CORE but at the same time building a new IDENTITY which matches the real person as closely as a glove fits a hand. This all requires great courage as in this extraordinary journey of self, all stand alone. The price of being an individual is that, although one may have friends and "comrades in arms", ultimately a person has to be entirely self-reliant. There are only two ways to go: one can be part of a COLLECTIVE (like the vast majority of life forms on the planet) or one can be an INDIVIDUAL but the price of that individuality is standing alone. This does demand courage and the person needs to deliberately undo the grip and stronghold of fear and doubt that everyone has in the face of the unknown. Self-reliance is the watchword here. As Ralph Waldo Emerson said in his essay entitled "Self-Reliance": "Be yourself; no base imitator of another but your best self. There is something you can do better than another."

It is impossible to live in a culture such as our own without developing an EGO and an IDEOLOGY and it is likely that these will stand in opposition to the EMERGENT SELF and its requirements. Therefore, the person will need to develop an IDEOLOGY based on new values and beliefs that match the evolving self rather than stand against it. This constitutes a real inner battle between the growing ENTITY OF SELF and the myriad of different people that exist in each of us, hidden away, who have their own private agenda where our lives are concerned. These are essentially the faces of the multiple roles we have created in ourselves to cope with living, none of which are truly us but who nonetheless jump up like wayward jack-in- the-boxes whenever we let our guard down. We have all had moments when something in us said or did the wrong thing, simply because at that particular moment our attention slipped and an unfortunate forgotten role managed to take over. This simply says that the developing life needs to live their own EVENTS OF LIFE rather than surrendering to a proxy self which is just a ghostly role rather than the real I AM. It rather begs the question what, at any time, is actually making use of our body and faculties? Who, actually, is in the driving seat of ourselves?

Fortunately, a person eventually arrives at a point where they have crossed the boundary; their decision regarding self has become irrevocable and there is no longer an option to turn back. The Inner Self is now fully AWAKE and the drive to go on is now a COMPULSION. The person will hold to a greater purpose regardless of price because the thought of turning back is anathema; the culture and ordinary life no longer holds any appeal. From now on, the reincarnated person no longer needs the prop of faith and has developed a surety of self. Beliefs are no longer aspired to; they are LIVED. (Truly, Belief and Faith are just staging posts along the development journey which can be shed once a person's experience takes them into the actuality of creational life – a crude analogy of this is that in a physical body, a person doesn't believe they need to eat, they know they must eat in order to survive). Once the true Self is fully awake and conscious, the death of the physical body is no longer to be feared because the person is secure in the knowledge that real things in them that are able to survive death have already crystallised. Furthermore, awakening to ACTUALITY and the re-establishment of natural connections and abilities inherent in the human design, including the higher possibilities of the brain itself leads to not just an appreciation of an enhanced life to come but also to a greater value-added life now.

Chapter 9:
3rd After-life Settings

THE CONSIDERATION OF THE 2ND REINCARNATION

The person is now engaged in multiple life returns in which aspects of self are either remade or remodelled according to need, hopefully with the goal of bringing the life closer to the Entity of Self. If this is not the case, because the life has drifted away from its CORE origins yet still managed to crystallise around something durable, say a powerful cultural ideology, the person then experiences the onset of a repetitional life in the form of roles. It is worth noting here that most of the people we see around us today have probably reincarnated; there are very few "newbies" simply because although the Planet once needed input from Creation and local constellations to power organic life, she has now accumulated so much she probably no longer has to rely on the Spawning.

Ideally, the person starts to experience a series of lives as a schooling and a learning, with each new lifetime bringing greater scope of experience and opportunity to grow to the real self. This is obviously what is vaguely hinted at in the Buddhist and Hindu idea of Karma, in which the sum of a person's actions and experience in one life determines their future in their next existence but the truth that is missed here is that the criteria governing this is Planetary and Creational purpose; ultimately, the life needs to make itself upon the ACTUALITY of how Life happens rather than on a vague emotional hope that things will turn out right in the end.

As a background to this, one needs to appreciate that a person experiences just one culture and that could be just one of a whole series of different cultures which themselves form part of a civilisation; a life could have had many hundreds of lives previously, in a continuum stretching back to their origins. The life can then

THE LIVING EVENT OF THE HUMAN LIFE

carry a residue of these into their next physical life.

It is entirely possible that the person's previous experience has eventually brought them on a journey back to the original EVENT OF SELF, with all its inherent promise. This will encourage the person to seek a physical embodiment that will facilitate a singular stance and purpose throughout their life – something that will magnify and allow the actuality of self to grow. Ultimately, the person is seeking the opportunity to purpose their life in such a way that they become the master of it rather than living a life in which they are blown hither and thither by circumstance.

It is at this point that the person enters the higher event of Reincarnation, henceforth referred to as "the Pitching Life". Up until this point the life has been "yawing" in the way an aircraft or a boat will sway side to side in a storm, as an example. Even if the person has purpose and direction in their life, they are still likely to vacillate and they can still "fall asleep" and settle back into a life of roles. However, the Pitching life is a CORE life (all previous lives are yawing) and its most outstanding feature is "Way"; those with "pitching lives" have reached a turning point in the ACTUALITY of life – this is a pivotal life that allows a person to step outside of planetary and begin to build embodiments that can exist at higher levels.

The Way, which has been previously touched on, begins when a person starts to realise there's something different to cultural life, they WAKE UP to the greater possibility of SELF and begin to exhibit PITCHING behaviour. Pitching is proactive in the same way as a baseball pitcher initiates play; in a word, the person has begun to take control of the direction of their event of life. The pitching life is aimed at bringing oneself to the fullest fulfilment of one's promise of life and it offers the chance to step outside of one's family tree (the Transient line) and become a FREE RADICAL. (This requires further explanation as generally the term "free radical" has rather negative connotations; here it means a person has started to become the Entity of Self and to fulfil the original Creational promise of unique individuality, as opposed to being part of a COLLECTIVE. It is important to understand that virtually all life forms on the planet – for example, bees, wildebeest, cattle – behave as collectives rather than individuals. Even the culture we live in, which prides itself on self-expression, actually only exhibits collective behaviour).

The Pitching life offers a hitherto impossible freedom, in that this life has greater freedom of choice and can choose an era in which to be born; things in the person have by now crystallised to a degree that makes them less subject to diminishment whilst in the astral and ethereal domains. These people will be looking for a future life that will allow them to continually build up their Greater Self and become the Entity of Self in the fullest possible fashion.

THE LIVING EVENT OF THE HUMAN LIFE

THE CONSIDERATIONS OF THE SECOND TRANSFORMATION

In this it is important to realise that humans live in a physical world and are for the most part entirely unaware of the vast panoply of electro-magnetic life around them. This can only be lightly touched upon here as the subject is vast, but suffice it to say that electro-magnetic attendances of the Planet are as diverse and wonderful as the great array of physical life-form we see around us.

As the person develops and becomes closer to the ACTUALITY of SELF, they begin to attract an entourage of much finer electrical life forms which very much wish to associate with humans but are unable to if people lack the right CONTENT. This entourage may include elemental life forms, healing elementals, Earth life (explained previously) and finer energies such as Silver and Gold force, to name but a few. Some of this attendance may attach itself to the developing life and be "cocooned" in them awaiting rebirth in the same way that insect life can be kept safe in a cocoon until circumstances are right for it to be born. "Cocoons" can also include entire personas that can be locked away as a micro-signal in blood or the aura of a person awaiting the opportunity to subsume another personality; perhaps the most extraordinary of these is the case of Dorothy Eady who was born in London in 1903 and at the age of three fell downstairs and was knocked unconscious (though some stories claim she was pronounced dead). Whatever the case, when she recovered her character had changed completely, her speech patterns were significantly different and she kept asking to be taken "home". A year later, when her nonplussed parents took her to the British Museum, she pointed to a photo of the temple of Seti

1 and stated that that was her home.

Dorothy later claimed to be the reincarnation of a priestess of Isis named Bentreshyt who had become pregnant with Seti's child and taken her own life as a consequence. Eventually, Dorothy lived out her life in Egypt under the name of Ommseti (literally the woman of Seti). All this could be dismissed as the ravings of a lunatic, if it were not for the extraordinary details of her former life at the Temple that she shared with archaeologists working at the Temple of Seti 1 and which were subsequently proven to be accurate by their work. This is an extraordinary case and suggests that other lives can "piggy-back" on another person awaiting the opportunity to take over their physical body; this appears to be exactly what happened to Dorothy Eady.[1]

Dorothy Eady

Alongside natural planetary attendances such as Elementals and Earth life, the person may have accumulated connections to Antiquity and Ancient Embodiments which also gather around them in preparation for their next physical appearance. It must be remembered that just as a person's aura contains the record of their life and daily thought processes, so the Planet's electro- magnetic fields (sometimes called the Akashic records) contains a record of

---

[1] https://en.wikipedia.org/wiki/Dorothy_Eady

every great civilisation and event that has occurred upon her. Some people, perhaps especially those who have experienced a long continuum of reincarnations that stretch back a long way into Antiquity, have a special affinity with events from history and these may form strong attachments to previous times.

Regrettably, few people recall previous lives but it is certainly true that connections made previously that are REAL and ACTUAL are likely to survive the death of the physical body and remain "cocooned" in the person until the right opportunity for manifestation occurs. It is also possible that there are aspects of Antiquity that are looking for the opportunity to re-occur in the future, because everything wants to live, including ancient cultures; therefore, they will be happy to put themselves in service to someone who is Way and is going somewhere. The person who has reached this stage in the journey towards the Entity of Self may also have hidden, locked away "passengers" inside them that will remain dormant until their next physical life provides them with the right opportunity. Some of these may come from a person's transient tree and some will be transcendental and specifically have to do with above planetary connections that the life has made in their previous physical existence. For us, living a long way from the core of Creation, this means initially connections to Sun and Solar level, which are the first point of ascension for us.

In addition, if the person has had associations with Earth life and structures before their previous life ended, these may carry through into the Afterlife. Earth life is a complicated subject which requires much study but as it is essentially planetary bound and cannot exist outside the Planet it is keen to offer service to humans of the right calibre (that is, humans whose lives are actually purposeful) and this will continue into the person's afterlife.

THIRD AFTERLIFE SETTINGS

Perhaps this is the moment to further explore the subject of REBORNS. At this point, the reader will recall that reborns have, over a series of lives, acquired a CONTENT that has to do with a specific domain, say music, mathematics, art to name but a few. In this way, they have surrendered their ENTITY OF SELF and NATURAL IDENTITY and crystallised around a particular area of expertise rather than their own CORE. They may have excelled in their chosen domain and it is certainly true that the **event of Content Singularity** invites Reborn process. It is certainly true that the Planet herself cherishes reborns because by and large they carry the unique content that she needs to reach her next stage of evolution. (A word about evolution; it is important to understand that the planet is looking to refine and develop just as humans should be. Evolution in this sense has to do with a process that allows refinement and ascension rather than just an arbitrary process. The Planet is looking for a CONTENT that will allow her to become stellar – in this sense evolution is PURPOSEFUL rather than arbitrary. This is the truth that Darwinism seems to have missed.

It is important to realise that the reborn process will not allow a person to rise above planetary; by dedicating themselves to this path they have unconsciously committed themselves to planetary purpose and their future is inextricably linked to that purpose- if the Planet fails, they fail. However, although it is difficult for a Reborn to re-enter the Reincarnation process by losing their adhesion to CONTENT and starting back in pursuit of the Entity of Self, it is not impossible. Equally, a person on a Reincarnation journey can slip into a reborn process. The EVENT of CONTENT SINGULARITY invites REBORN process and this can occur even in a Way person if they simply accumulate content without a purpose. This is why it is vital that the "pitching" life consciously

THE LIVING EVENT OF THE HUMAN LIFE

builds a purpose of life as a fulcrum for everything they do. It is also important to realise that both reincarnate and reborn can fall to different species if they fail to maintain what they are. Whichever path one is on, maintenance of self is essential because nothing is guaranteed. There are certainly examples of animals that display uncannily human attitude, suggesting that they may have previously been human but lacked the right number of "points" to fuel a human body this time around.

THE CONSIDERATIONS OF REBORN AGAIN

For those who have been acquiring specific content to do with a particular discipline or area of expertise rather than in pursuit of the Entity of Self, there is a tendency in time to develop genius and for the person to pick up the threads of a previous life at a younger and younger age. Children like this demonstrate an uncanny precocity in the discipline or area of expertise they have previously devoted their lives to; from the moment of their birth, they are pre-set on a particular path and are able to be divinatory to previous content carried through from earlier lives. The child prodigy Soborno Isaac Bari is an outstanding example of this.

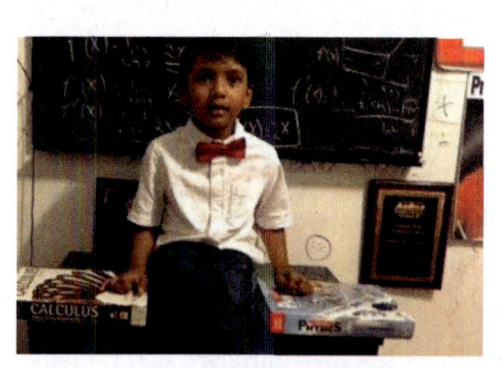

Soborno Isaac Bari

THIRD AFTERLIFE SETTINGS

Eventually, the REBORN path becomes a continuous CONTINUUM in the sense of a coherent progression or sequence of Events leading to the same outcome.

Reborns are conscious within the sphere of their personal expertise, even though they lack the identity that a reincarnating life carries. The passage of possibly many lives practising their skills has allowed them to finesse their "art" (not necessarily in painting or sculpture but in any planetary domain they have surrendered to), and it is this background that allows them to develop genius in their chosen discipline. At the same time, the accumulated content and cognisance of previous lives allows the reborn to start to activate higher aspects of their mental domain from an early age. This permits the person's higher centres – which are to do with the higher aspects of the brain – to start to influence the ACTUALITY of the life. This leads to an Eminent Content and Embodiment in the life of the reborn person, which allows them to divine higher knowledge and understanding about their chosen area of work and expertise. To clarify, Eminent is a state that has to do with the Human head and the unlocked potential of the Brain. It will be difficult for the reader to grasp the fact that in its present state of development the human makes minimal use of the extraordinary possibility of the brain. Currently, the human mostly uses the brain in a planetary fashion but higher usage of this most remarkable instrument allows a person to connect to Solar level and to become CONSCIOUS rather than simply AWAKE. Rather than being simply connected to the Astral Domain, the person is joined to the Animated and Higher Ethereal domains and this initiates a greater connection to the Alive. For those who are able to see into the unseen worlds and particularly the electro-magnetic fields around the human head, this would most definitely cause different STRUCTURES to appear in the vicinity of the Head which could be seen. (An interesting aside here is that many of the elaborate headdresses worn in antiquity and specifically in the regalia of royalty actually reflect structure already constructed magnetically by the Head itself). With respect to reborns, this in turn will lead to great facility and expertise within their chosen discipline as well as greater vitalisation and dynacism, but won't necessarily help them in their day-to-day lives – many geniuses, such as Beethoven and Mozart, have been entirely inept at managing ordinary living.

Reborn knowledge carries a heightened illumination and greater consciousness within their chosen area of expertise; long-term reborns are also able to tap into the great continuum of Antiquity and gain cognisance of the deep knowledge of hitherto lost cultures and civilisations, some of which may even contain inert alien memory.

This is clearly a controversial claim, but there is unquestionably evidence that alien races have played a considerable part in human affairs and possibly even the genetic "hot-housing" of the Human Race. This has come to light especially in the past fifty years or so, with authors such as Robert Temple, whose book "The Sirius Mystery"[2] explores the extraordinary knowledge of the Dogon[3] tribe in Africa, whose esoteric and detailed understanding of the Sirius system stretches back into the distant past. The Dogon always insisted that their deep and accurate astronomical knowledge of the Sirius system (which they knew for many hundreds of years prior to modern scientific discovery) was given to them by alien visitors that they revered and founded their culture upon.

---

[2] The Sirius Mystery Robert K. G. Temple. 1976.St Martins Press

[3] https://en.wikipedia.org/wiki/Dogon_people

The fact that they knew details about Sirius – such as the fact that it is a binary star and the mathematics of its orbit – long before

Two examples of Dogon ceremonial masks

these things could be verified by modern astronomers and their telescopes, can only be ascribed to the Dogon's claim that they received this knowledge from visitors from Sirius itself.

Reborns, particularly after many lifetimes of dedicated service to their chosen disciplines, have an elemental outplay par excellence – the reader will recall that the elemental aspect of self is the "doing" aspect of human life as opposed to the inner "being" of a person. For this reason, it is hardly surprising that planetary elementals, whose entire purpose of life is the maintenance and eventual evolution of the Planet, should have a particular interest in reborns. This will accentuate their instincts to develop – the instinct is a powerful link between the Planet and organic life and in humans carries a purity of purpose that over-rides cultural considerations. The instinctive centre is hard-wired to the urge to survive – one only has to think of the speed with which it gets a person out of the path of say, an oncoming bus, long before they themselves actually compute what is happening.

Elemental life form is dedicated to the purposes of the Planet and her drive to refine and evolve; the Planet is looking to accumulate the best possible CONTENT because it is this which

THE LIVING EVENT OF THE HUMAN LIFE

will allow her to become a star. (Stars, like planets, require life form, but that life form will be more refined and rarefied than that which is needed further down Creation). All life form exists to fuel its place of origin by making the right connections to that which feeds it – all organic life here, flowers, trees, animals and even humans, are part of a great machine that the Planet created to gather the right kind of sun, solar and stellar forces to herself.

Everything natural here is part of the Planet's produce, and it either maintains her or helps her on her ascensional journey. Eventually, she will shed that which no longer serves her purpose, but she will keep that which does and take good care of it, rather like a lady who keeps her most special jewels safe. Reborns can play a special part in the Planet's future evolution because they can have superlative CONTENT untainted by personality. They are bound to the Planet and will never follow the same path as a person seeking their entity of self, but they do have an important part to play here. They live in a continuous continuum of connections with Afterlife pipelines to a greater event, that is the Planet's evolution. They are not "free radical" like those pursuing their Core self, but they are part of a great collective that stretches back into history and forward into the future and it is likely they dwell and abide with **Elemental Presence** even though they themselves are probably not aware of it.

THIRD AFTERLIFE SETTINGS

THE CONSIDERATIONS OF RESURRECTION

Reincarnation relates to the Planetary life and the planetary purposes of life with the possible option of being part of a future refined human race at Star level; reincarnation does not ascend above planetary level, but there is a promise of Resurrection implicit in the Pitching life mentioned earlier. This is an ascensional life event which allows a person to set their sights upon a far higher level than planetary and to build containments in themselves that will allow this to happen. This is the original promise of life held by the Making, prior to Spawning (see column 1) and it includes the taking possession of the Entity of Self and setting out upon an ascensional journey towards the upper echelons of Creation itself. It is a lonely journey because it demands self-reliance of a very high order as everything has to be by one's own making.

This includes the Conscious Retention of Human Identity whilst offsetting and standing in denial of wrongful content and possession; the identity must be tailor-made to truthfully and genuinely reflect the individuality, as intimately as a glove fits a hand. Also, having already resurrected human abilities that have long since been dormant, the person needs to activate previously unused areas of the Head Domain (the higher possibility of the brain) as a starting point for the creational journey. It must be understood that currently, the human brain is asleep to its own possibility, in a "third world condition", and it requires connection to the right order of fuel to fulfil its potential.

In the ascensional journey beyond planetary, the person must

THE LIVING EVENT OF THE HUMAN LIFE

use the Solar as a launching platform, which means elevating oneself to the realms of the Animated (the domain beyond Astral and Ethereal) and gathering the right kind of connections and knowledge to make oneself upon it. At the same time, one has to bear the scars and repairs of one's previous lives, for no one emerges from the battle field of planetary life unscathed. At the same time, a person must consciously retain human identity and have a humility in the face of the higher and compassion towards that which has not yet reached the same point in the journey.

To sum up, the ascensional event is the ultimate proposition for any individual life or species. From the human perspective, Creation has clearly built a ladder that is going somewhere and it is possible to build embodiments and containments at many levels in a continuum by virtue of one's own works, always remembering that what one builds has to be founded upon Creational purpose itself. In a way, Resurrection is to do with a transformative form of life that is really the start of a new genus in the sense of a unique class of things that has common characteristics. It takes a person beyond the idea of a work of life (previously agreed to) to a WAY of Life.

Chapter 10:
First Thereafter Event

Life beyond the planetary; the Thereafter life; Resurrection; the Occult and the Esoteric; Alien interference in the Human Affair; Living or Serving Life; the Maintenance Life

THE LIVING EVENT OF THE HUMAN LIFE

THE CONSIDERATIONS OF THE THEREAFTER LIFE

This relates to the possibility of future existence outside the Solar System and even the possibility of this is something rare and high which hardly anyone in recorded history has aspired to, let alone achieved. It must be appreciated that the so-called "heavens" of established religions, if they exist at all are most likely located in the Ethereal realms of the Planet and are theoretically the reward for a lifetime adhesion to a particular dogma rather than something that relates to the emancipation of the Entity of Self. Indeed, given the collective nature of organised religions and dogma, they are COLLECTIVE in nature rather than offering INDIVIDUAL liberation.

In ACTUALITY, planetary experience and understanding (based on the study of natural law) supports the notion that Creation is a practical affair; the latest data from the Hubble telescope tells us that it appears to be expanding at a rate of over 163,000 miles per hour and if this is the case then eventually all that STRUCTURE is going to require LIFE to service and maintain it.

It has already been inferred that the Planet herself is working towards becoming a star and that she will require LIFE FORM of a more refined order to achieve this and them maintain herself. This is the PROMISE of the TRANSIENT TREES, if they are able to meet the criteria, and in the fullness of time this will no doubt occur. However, for those willing to pay the price it is possible to follow an ascensional path that grants pre-evolutionary access to the stars and even beyond.

This is the fulfilment of the promise of the Entity of Self and really means a planned return to one's Creational origins; it means responding to the uplift and calling of a higher domain of life and event by using this life as a starting platform.

It is not a question of faith or belief but begins with building higher mental structures in oneself that connect to increasingly greater octaves. These constitute higher embodiments which are able to manifest in miniature inside oneself whilst on the Planet. These embodiments would have a sympathetic resonance with their point of origin; in a sense a person is building a deposit account in the higher realms that one can only access when one leaves the Planet.

Above and beyond the planetary realm, the first consideration has to be the fulfilment of one's Sun and Solar promise. This promise is implicit in the possibility of activating higher functions of the Human Brain, long dormant (for it has long been appreciated that the Brain is truly the last undiscovered continent).

It is fascinating to note the extraordinary similarities scientists are beginning to notice between the brain and Creation itself, which perhaps gives an inkling of the extraordinary human possibility.

However, to be brief, the activation of the Sun and Solar domains of life is vital because the Creational journey begins at Solar level – remember, it was remarked earlier that our solar system is the equivalent of a single cell. Just as the semi-permeable membrane of a cell inside the body controls the passage of what gets in and out of it, the Solar system controls what gets in or out of its own domains. It is possible to reach a development point where the Solar System itself can no longer contain the person and they have to move on; rather like the young adult whose family, with love, affection but a

THE LIVING EVENT OF THE HUMAN LIFE

tinge of relief suggests its now time they set up on their own!

The journey of human development begins at Planetary and moves to Solar via a Sun Core attendance. (It is interesting that so-called Sun worship stretches far back into Antiquity and is often derided as "primitive" but perhaps it actually derives from a genuine human recognition of the Sun as a higher Entity, without which life here would very swiftly blink out). To appreciate this Work, a person does need to understand that, just as a human is far more than just a physical body, so is the Sun far more than a nearly perfect ball of hot plasma. Also, it is important to broaden and deepen one's views (which are inevitably a product of one's education and are limited by its parameters) and realise that just because life on a planet and at this level of Creation is carbon-based that does not necessarily mean that life elsewhere is not electro-magnetic or plasma based.

To return to our main theme: it is possible to crystallise structures in the human body that resonate with creational structures beyond this particular Solar System, starting with Sun Core attendance (in the form of higher life forms which would choose to associate with human beings who are working to fulfil the promise of being human).

As has been previously mentioned, Life in Creation at all levels has only three options – to live, to serve or to maintain. Therefore, the journey from Sun Core to Solar Core requires a person to put on a pair of overalls and join the "Maintenance Team". The next step beyond Solar Core life is the Constellational affair but a person must not forget that they are building a tower that stretches from planetary to beyond and like in a house each floor is the platform for the next – it is foolish to build on unreliable foundations. (Christ refers to this in Matthew 7 24 -26, when he speaks of a man who builds his house on rock rather than a foolish man who builds his house on sand). This is why it is again and again so important to check out one's works and purpose against the infallible gyroscopic action of planetary and creational law. Not only does this order of work produce personal uplift, it also generates VITALITY in a person, which is one of the main features of the Animated life, itself essential for any who wish to rise above Sun level.

THE LIVING EVENT OF THE HUMAN LIFE

THE CONSIDERATIONS OF RESURRECTION/ RE-EMBODIMENT

Resurrection is a profound and difficult subject that is not commonly understood today; it is also very difficult not to see it through the prism of orthodox Christian teachings. Esoterically, it means that, as happens with cataleptics, the body may appear to be rigid and to all intents and purposes dead. The person themselves is absent but at some point, they return to their physical life and recommence their life journey. This also appears to happen for people in near death experiences and is often cathartic and constitutes an epiphany for the person concerned. It is frequently **transformative** and marks the beginning of an entirely new life for the person; in some cases, it seems to herald the onset of psychic abilities, in some it seems to drive a person to entirely different pursuits, particularly helping others, that are quite different to the kind of activities they did before. For many people it seems to mark a point in their life when they become less driven by ego and more intent on helping others. For those who keep the memory of their experience, they entirely lose any fear they may have of death itself. It is as if the experience causes a concentration of the core Entity of Self and helps the person to be more naturally focussed and less likely to succumb to the influence of culture.

It is also worth pointing out that there are centuries old traditions in India that insist that Jesus did in fact survive the Crucifixion and went on to continue his ministry in India. At the end of the nineteenth century Hazrat Ahmad, the founder of the Ahmadiyya Muslim Jamaat, wrote a treatise in Urdu (subsequently translated into "Jesus in India" for Western readers) which argues that Jesus went on to live a revered and religious life in India after his supposed death. He also remarks that after the Resurrection, the Gospel of Mark refers to Jesus needing to eat, drink and sleep, which is hardly necessary if one does not have a physical body!

THE LIVING EVENT OF THE HUMAN LIFE

THE OCCULT AND THE ESOTERIC

In this section it is important to get some understanding of the word "occult", which unfortunately has a very bad press in this culture which tends to associate the words with dark practices and the whole domain of witchcraft and sinister goings on (the famous horror film based on Dennis Wheatley's "The Devil Rides Out"[1] is a prime example of this).

"Esoteric", a word equally misunderstood (the dictionary defines it as knowledge that is only likely to be understood by people with very specialised knowledge and interests) can be described as the hidden and generally unknown mechanics of something (but mostly unknown and hidden because people do not understand the natural laws). "Occult" is the energy that passes through the Esoteric, in the same way as the mechanics of a car is esoteric, the process by which it comes "alive" and is driven is Occult. Esoteric knowledge leads a person to be able to construct a pentagram or a triangle which are both symbols of highly occult processes.

In considering the subject of the thereafter, it is very important to understand the connected power and influence of primary Occultism as well as the esoteric practices that allow a person to harvest the right energies from the Occult. This is not a sinister practise because symbols like the pentagram, the Seal of Solomon, the cosmic triangle (to name but a few) are natural, planetary, solar or higher in origin and connect to higher processes that a person

---

[1] Wheatley, Dennis (2007) [1935]. The Devil Rides Out. Wordsworth Editions. ISBN 978-1840225433

needs to fuel their ascensional journey. Explained simply, if a person makes a study of say, the Cosmic Triangle (just like if they take the trouble to study the Law of Two and its deeper meaning) first of all they start to understand the mechanics of the symbol. Later they begin to connect in a small way with the occult processes that the cosmic triangle contains. (One would not want to connect in a big way because these are extraordinarily powerful and the result would probably be literally incandescent!)

There is also considerable power in the combined Thought Form movement in Collectives. The collective power of millions of Moslems praying five times a day while facing Mecca or the power of the Roman Catholic Mass is enormous and one has to wonder what that is actually channelled into. It is certainly not channelled into the individual CORES of the people who devote themselves to those religions so what is it actually fuelling? There is a Saviour effect on the notions and ideas of a collective which is exemplified by the Christian belief that Christ died for everyone's sins and that his death is an astral purge that wipes out everybody's wrong manufacture. (In actuality, the death of Christ, who was clearly a very high and illumined person, was meant to clean the planet's astral domains which were filthy and polluted from the appalling legacy of the Roman Empire rather than to allow individual people to abnegate responsibility for their own petty misdemeanours). Unfortunately, in a Collective, everyone or everything thinks, feels and behaves the same and serves the same purpose (just like a hive of bees) so in a true collective the Saviour notion would unquestionably work.

There are other controversial points to be made here. In the past fifty years or so, it has become increasingly obvious to any thinking person that studies ancient history, that the human race

THE LIVING EVENT OF THE HUMAN LIFE

has been the subject of alien interference on a number of past occasions. Even the Bible, often a "chancy" point of reference, refers to the "fallen angels" who had sex with human women thus creating the Nephilim and there are a multitude of events from history that suggest that mostly benign aliens have tried to "hot-house" human culture and fast track human evolution. "The Sirius Mystery" (By Robert Temple) previously mentioned, describes in some detail how the Dogon tribe got their esoteric knowledge of Sirius from alien visitors from Sirius who were themselves partially aquatic (they had to spend a lot of their time in water) and, to human eyes, extraordinarily repulsive!

In "The Sirius Mystery", Robert Temple makes reference to a book called "Intelligent Life in the Universe" by Carl Sagan and I.S. Shklovski[2], that describes "some fascinating creatures credited with founding the Sumerian civilisation (which sprang up out of nowhere as many Sumerian archaeologists will unhappily admit)" ("The Sirius Mystery" Page 90). They were "described in a classical account by Alexander Polyhistor as amphibious. He says they were happier if they could go back into the sea at night and return to the dry land in the daytime. All the accounts describe them as being semi-demons, personages or animals endowed with reason, but they are never called gods. They were "super-human" in knowledge and length of life and they eventually returned in a ship 'to the gods' carrying with them representatives of the fauna of earth" (Page 90 Sirius Mystery). It is also interesting to note that many Assyrian figures are portrayed as half fish (the mermaids and mermen of legend come to mind here) and even Ancient China claimed that its original founders were fish-tailed. Cult images from the worship of

---

[2] Intelligent Life in the Universe Paperback. Carl Sagan, I. S. Shklovskii. 1984 Holden Day. ISBN 0816279136

Isis often show her and her spouse as fish-tailed. There is a wealth of evidence of alien interference in human history documented in "The Sirius Mystery" should the reader be interested in pursuing this line of inquiry.

Stories which explain the true arising of cultures like Sumeria, together with the extraordinary evidence for high cultures and civilisations gathered by authors like Graham Hancock and open-minded archaeologists like John West leave the reader with little doubt that the paradigm of history presented by orthodox historians is entirely inadequate in its explanation of human origins.

To return to the matter in hand, there is an abundance of evidence that there has been alien influence in human affairs and that this has had an evolutionary knock-on effect or affect or both. Not only does this postulate the inter-breeding of planetary life form with Aliens (possibly with a view to accelerating human development) but it also opens up the argument that some of our technologies and even our religious dogmas are actually hand-me-downs from a superior race of being than our own. This would clearly account for the fact that the Human Race appears to have a far greater acumen, intelligence and possibility than any other Planetary life form and it also accounts for the fact that humans have an ascensional possibility which the other fauna of earth simply don't have; they are locked into the Planet and her purposes and their evolution is linked directly to that. We share 99% of our DNA with chimpanzees but that 1% difference between us makes for a staggering divergence of possibility and its tempting to conclude that in some distant epoch some superior race tampered with our genetics just a little in an attempt to change our species and life on our Planet forever.

THE LIVING EVENT OF THE HUMAN LIFE

Alongside Alien and other life form practices (some of which have been inculcated into religion itself) it is most important to consider Elemental involvement and Event in the human story. This is an enormous subject which really requires an entire book (if not several books) devoted to its explanation and exploration, if the reader is to truly understand the importance of elemental life on the Planet. However, constrictions of time mean that only a cursory (but vital) explanation can be offered here.

The reader must understand that in the beginning, the Planet was born from two elements (magma or matter) and fire; however, as the building blocks of Creational structure are constructed of three things (carbon, oxygen and nitrogen being the obvious example) something else, from a higher octave, was required in addition and that was Sun Elemental in the form of a plasma – the Sun is almost like a Bank Manager that gives the Planet a substantial loan to build her business.

The Planet's initial life form was great cone-shaped elementals and these vast entities still exist today and are essential to the reciprocal maintenance of life on the Planet. Interestingly, the transient nature of life on the Planet (not just in humans but also in other organic life forms) has its origins here, in the great maintenance cone elementals of antiquity. There is a connected superiority of Elemental life here on the Planet; as time went on, other Elementals generated from the original cone-shaped maintainers (just as evolutionary leaps have happened in the species of Earth, say from cold-blooded life forms to warm- blooded). Today there are elementals that maintain organic life, often a specific species and even Earth life (which are unseen life forms that humans have known as elves, gnomes, sylphs and a host of others) which lives in and cares for flora life. This has been touched on previously and no doubt the cynical will scoff at the idea that such electro-magnetic life forms exist, but the diligent and open-minded reader will find an abundance of evidence for this if they care to look.

A person does need to regularly remind themselves that generally the processes that govern the Planet are thought of as at best an arbitrary evolutionary event; what must be appreciated is that we are living in a GREAT MACHINE with its own purposes, and that everything we see around us serves a practical purpose. Elemental life comes with a wide variety of function and regulates everything upon the Planet including the seasons, the weather and much more.

It is also worth pointing out that, as well as having Planetary Being, humans have Elemental content themselves, and this allows them to deal with Elementals naturally and without ritual (looking at human history, it is clear that religion and a variety of esoteric groups, including the Druids, have compelled certain elemental forces to serve them – if a person is following a natural purpose of life, then this is quite unnecessary because the Elementals would quite happily help them).

Being ELEMENTAL, the human already has the possibility of Sun level initiation. This was a core aspect of Egyptian religious practice that was only possible because the human, unlike most other planetary life forms, has sun level possibility.

For this very important reason, it is vital for a person who wishes to develop beyond planetary and to build embodiments higher up the creational bar, to rebuild and reprocess their Elemental parts. In the past, religion and schools have tended to neglect the elemental nature of ourselves and concentrate on the

THE LIVING EVENT OF THE HUMAN LIFE

BEING (the inner life); prayer, contemplation, dwelling and such practices are all meat and drink to the Being life but living is about a correct balance between the inner and the outer life with due respect paid to both.

Everything in Creation works to a balance and there should be a state of reciprocal maintenance between the BEING and the ELEMENTAL in which the BEING powers the ELEMENTAL and the ELEMENTAL powers the BEING. The Elemental in us should gather the right kind of CONTENT for the inner life but without the right kind of education (a "Way" education based on natural law) the Elemental can only gather transitory cultural ROLES and the inner life has to subsist on an inadequate diet that does not nourish the person's CORE.

Building elemental and earth life connections is very important on the journey towards the Entity of Self because both elemental and earth life are a vital part of the human promise of life at planetary level and as such are essential to a person's planetary PURPOSE. These high- level planetary functionaries are able to assist the human in their development life should the person make the right signals in themselves. Elemental association ceases at Solar level because the Solar System in its function as an individual cell is creational in purpose and is the launching platform for a person's ascensional path. For this reason, elemental influence is terminated at the point of Entity of Self possession; at this moment the Planet and her entourage can only wish the person "bon voyage" and wave good-bye!

However, to fully arrive at this point a person needs to gather CONTENT from the Animated realms (the highest level of the Solar System where the residue of what the ordinary person would consider gods live) and to make themselves upon that content. This is because, to grow beyond the Planetary you have to add something to yourself that is above planetary; everything in the end is subject to the creation law that "everything returns to the source of its arising". It must be noted that the Solar System, like the simple cell, has a double membrane enclosing it known as the Chromos and the Kronos – like in a simple cell, the Chromos keeps things in (and therefore limits the possibility of things), the Kronos allows things from higher to enter and therefore allows ascensional possibility. There must be an ongoing negotiation between the two regarding the need to cleave to planetary criteria and the need to evolute. It is entirely possible that it will take several lifetimes for the person who has managed to build a Sun level CORE to reach Solar and beyond; the life will continue to experience the great recycling and repossession of living physical life forms and will be subject to the ageing process within a planetary domain. Regrettably, there are no guarantees until one is above Solar, the laws of limitation and repossession still apply and a person can still fail to achieve their PURPOSE.

THE LIVING EVENT OF THE HUMAN LIFE

THE CONSIDERATIONS OF LIVING OR SERVING LIFE

For many, the religious view is that Life is the primary focus and that the structure in which it appears that is the Planet, the Sun, the Solar System and beyond, exists for the purposes of Life. In actuality, the opposite is true – structure came first and subsequently Creation realised it needed Life to serve and maintain it. An excellent example of this is the Pentagram, which is a STRUCTURE but which contains something LIVING – the Human – and together they have the most amazing possibility.

For this reason, a person's Purpose of Life must encompass living, serving or maintaining as a first principle – a life must be USEFUL in one or all three of these domains if it is to tread the ascensional path. This is the Creational rule of Living and it is perhaps difficult for the inhabitants of Planet Earth to appreciate that, given that the planet's unfortunate history has given rise to cultures that are entirely offset to planetary purpose.

The flora and fauna of earth are excellent examples of living and serving in that they live and they serve the Planet by acting as receivers for the kind of force, sun, solar, star or even beyond that she needs to make herself upon. It is a sobering thought to realise that every blade of grass, every beautiful flower, every insect, every life form from a rabbit to an elephant is a tailor-made antenna for something the Planet needs. Just as we need to take in energy to maintain our bodies and higher processes, the Planet needs to maintain herself and attract higher frequencies which will allow her to evolve- everything natural we see around us is planetary industry and technology at work gathering what the Planet needs to first of all maintain herself and then progress her purpose of life. The Planetary industry is no different to a cultural one in that it is designed to make a profit.

In aspiring to higher life form and purpose, a person must consider what function they wish to fulfil, it being certain that the liberality of life that exists here on the planet is unlikely to exist anywhere else in creation.

On the Planet, the repetition of lives as one tries to refine, correct wrong manufacture in oneself and build structure that has a permanence beyond planetary may be considered the Afterlife. Subsequently, the person has the option to push on through into the Thereafter Dominions. (The word "dominion" is significant here because it implies absolute control, no personal freedom other than that permitted by the parameters of the domain itself).

However, the higher a person ascends in Creation the fewer the Laws governing the level in which they find themselves; the Natural Laws change both in elevation and profound event and it is difficult to imagine, based at planetary level at present what this might actually mean for the EVENT of life. The only certainties are to fulfil the need to live, serve or maintain.

Certainly, a person needs to appreciate that here, at planetary level, one needs a physical body in order to live and grow, whereas the higher one ascends in Creation the fewer the laws and the more rarefied the form; certain qualities which only turn up here as a fuel – for example spirituality – are elsewhere living entities. Manifestation in an Alive form with connections becomes a possibility; equally, a person may find themselves living in the form of a collective with all that that implies. There is also the option of

THE LIVING EVENT OF THE HUMAN LIFE

returning to planetary level to do a DUTY if one wishes.

Living is accompanied by Serving the criteria as a Duty or dedicating oneself to master-ship of a specific domain.

The greater promise lies within the forever/wherever Army of Maintenance lives; this inevitably includes the need to serve as part of the agenda. This is the option that demands the greatest versatility and prowess and is also the option that demands the greatest degree of fluidity, range and prowess because, as in any building or structure, the Maintenance team has to be prepared to go anywhere.

Once the person becomes the living embodiment of the Entity of Self, they are starting to shed the parts of themselves which we recognise as "human" and it is perhaps unwise to make the excuse "I'm only human" in case something hears you and keeps you there! However, before a person can aspire to a service or maintenance life, they must live WHAT they are, in the same way as planetary life form is WHAT IT IS. Serving is a higher calling but it has to be founded on the Alive and Animated domains of greater life.

Clearly, Creation has both requirements and needs and these represent the Criteria on which a SERVICE life must be based; Criteria lead to Protocols which are the behaviours necessary to facilitate criteria.

FIRST THEREAFTER EVENT

THE CONSIDERATIONS OF A MAINTAINING LIFE

It is clear that Creation, although a most awesome place, is not perfect and suffers entropy, as a consequence of which MAINTAINERS are vital. This has a planetary parallel in that there is awesome engineering apparent in say, an extraordinary railway engine or railway line, but no matter how fantastic it is it requires an army of engineers to maintain and service it.

Maintainers can be likened to the Mechanic that lives in the engine, rather like the 1966 Science-fiction film "Fantastic Voyage", in which a submarine crew are shrunk to microscopic size in order to go into the body of an injured scientist to repair his damaged brain. The purpose of the Maintainers is to keep Creational process kept and held in order, to maintain and keep Structural continuance and strengthening and to uphold the core regulation of all life. (One only has to consider the intricate workings of the human body to understand how vital these three functions actually are).

Equally, to be able to guarantee oneself at this level, the life clearly needs to be a Self-Regenerating Entity, continually using the ways and means of Remake, in the same way that the human body tries to continually remake itself on the blueprint of its design. This plainly means self-maintenance as a first principle, the ongoing upholding of Contracts and Covenants and the essential upkeep of one's own connections and power. It is, after all, self-evident that if a person is unable to take responsibility for themselves and their own maintenance nothing higher is going to grant them access to the Regulation and Re-construction of Creational Life Event itself.

Appendix I

APPENDIX I

AFTERLIFE CHARTS

BEFORE LIFE
(From Origin to Birth)

Stage 1 — FROM ORIGIN TO PRE-LIFE

a. Making
1- The Elemental Being
2- The Planetary Being
3- The Creational Alive

b. Spawning
1- The Biology of Creation
2- The Rhythms and Ascent
3- Creational Bypass
4- Struggle as a Maintenance of Life

c. Actuality/Conscious ways
1- Finality as a Decision
2- Arrangement as a One-of-it
3- Tidal Influences
4- Life Lives

d. Pre-Conception
1- The non-religious luck of chance
2- The winning edge of Impossibility
3- Tidal Influences
4- The Natural Laws

Stage 2 — PRE-LIFE SETTINGS

a. Time
1- Origins
2- Antiquity
3- Modern

b. Place and Form
1- Yawning
2- Repetition
3- Re-occurrence
4- Pitching

c. As What?
1- Entity
2- A self
3- Something Else
4- Collective

d. Transience (connections)
1- Return to/of Kind
2- Runners (time)
3- Transcendental
4- Greater Self Connection

Stage 3 — CONCEPTION TO BIRTH

a. Conception
1- The Situation Event (the Cattle Farm)
2- The Attendances (Transient)
3- Duties and Service (Connections)

b. Quickening
1- Formation of Physical Body
2- The Occupation of a space for Life
3- The Fight for life within the Mother
4- The Truth and Passion of Life itself

c. From- Term to Birth
1- The 'Rite to Be'
2- Creational event in Physical Form
3- The 9 Month Rule
4- Lost Creational Event

d. The Newbie- (1st Life)
1- Initiation of Being Human
2- Installation of Being Elemental
3- The Mother and Greater Mother
4- Occultism of the Alive to Life

THE LIVING EVENT OF THE HUMAN LIFE

AFTERLIFE CHARTS

TRILOGY OF INITIAL LIVES
(Start of 1st life to ending of 2nd life)

Stage 4
1st PHYSICAL LIFE
(The Planetary Newbie)

a. Gender
1- Metamorphosis
2- Jumpers
3- Transient tree

b. Physicality
1- The Feelings of Close Self
2- Re-connection to Natural self
3- The Values of influence and power
4- Life within a living machine

c. Culture
1- The nearest culture
2- Tramway to expression
3- Compleation by ability
4- The Remnants of a predictable life

d. Transience (works of Entity)
1- Influence and persuasion
2- Pedigree and caste
3- Experience
4- Divination

Stage 5
1st AFTER-LIFE SETTINGS

Re-Birth
1- The Re-set Event
2- The What of self event
3- The Greater Human making

b. Re-Born
1- The Content life
2- Awakened with no Huminality
3- Born again with content as a maker
4- Life form as a planetary living

c. Transient Lines (Info Archives)
1- Transience and culture in conflict
2- Arising Origin and Pedigree
3- Losing Entity in place of Identity
4- Orthodoxy as a standard

d. End results (Info Archives)
1- Return to/of Kind
2- Runners (time)
3- One never really Dies
4- To End as against to Quit

Stage 6
2nd PHYSICAL LIFE

a. Re-Birth- 2nd Physical life as something
1- Previous lives and memory
2- Struggle as a definitive way to succeed
3- Can finish as an Ending Life

b. Re-Born (going on with content)
1- Re-connection to containments
2- Development within greater abilities
3- Commencement of content Academia
4- Returns to self at an earlier age

c. Elemental Involvement (Info Archives)
1- Planetary Elemental event
2- The Earth Life involvement
3- Reborn Attendees
4- Divinatory Beginnings

d. Differences of Each (Info Archives)
1- Generalities and Specialisation
2- Autistic denial
3- Occupational Preferences
4- Specific Personal requirements

THE CYCLES OF CONTINUOUS PLANETARY LIFE

(Starts at 3rd physical life to a possible unlimited, unknown or untimed ending life)

page 3

Stage 7	Stage 8	Stage 9
2nd AFTER LIFE SETTINGS	**3rd PHYSICAL LIFE**	**3rd AFTER LIFE SETTINGS**
a. Re-Incarnational Event	a. The Continuous Revolution	a. Re-incarnation
1- The Roles of life and the Self	1- The Replay of Self in another life	1- Multiple Life Returns
2- The continuation of where it left off	2- Rise and Fall of Life event	2- The event of self Returns
3- The start of the rise and fall lives	3- Purpose and Loss	3- The Pitching Life
b. Re-born Continues	b. The new difficulty of Self	b. Re-Born again
1- Reverse time to naturalisation	1- Unsettlement of the Inner life	1- Tending with time to Genius of Life
2- Kinetic involvement	2- Wrong Manufacture	2- Conscious without Human identity
3- Occultisation of Content	3- Entity Identity and Earth Life	3- Elemental involvement at Self Origin
4- Importation of entity of self	4- Development and Resolution	4- Becomes a continuous Continuum
c. Transformational	c. The Way of the New Genius	c. Transformation
1- Gender Jumpers	1- The Mental life development	1- Cocoons and Sleepers
2- Species leapers	2- The Maintenance of the self	2- Occurrences
3- Culture only	3- Living connections to the Work	3- Earth life structures
4- Anchors and Travellers	4- The contest for the Entity of self	4- Reborns to Re-incarns and vice versa
d. Activity out of Settings (Info Archives)	d. The Greater Order and Criteria	d. Resurrection
1- Earth Life involvement	1- The Higher life activities	1- The Possible event of any life
2- Elementalisation	2- The swap of Identity and Entity	2- Conscious Retention of Human Identity
3- Planetary Domain Life form	3- Ego, Ideology and Green-man	3- Manifestation of Higher Life
4- Inception of special roles	4- Resolve and Commitment	4- Ascension life event

APPENDIX II

APPENDIX Ii

REBUILDING AND RECONSTRUCTING OUR ELEMENTAL NATURE (VIRSEL: ELEMENTAL PART 2)

For the purposes of this book, it is important the reader understands the Elemental aspect of themselves as well as **the Being** side of themselves and the way the two interact and build.

Imagine the two, which are the inner and outer aspects of a person sitting within a circle which has spokes like a wheel. There are two crosses inside the circle, one a physical cross, one Solar, one electric, one magnetic. Planetary Content (Being) and Elemental Content both sit at the centre or HUB of the Wheel and between the two an electro-magnetic EVENT occurs. (It is important to understand that the Human works on alternating current rather than direct current – our lungs act like a dynamo, drawing energy and air in on an in breath, pushing it out when we breathe out. The human blood is arterial and venal, we have two sides to our brains which currently appear to perform different functions, and so forth).

In the Human, the Elemental inclination is mostly towards the electrical on its way out; it needs the energy to go out and DO. When it comes back to the inner hub of the person, there is an exchange of Contents between the **Being life** and the **Elemental life** which should allow the **Inner life** to grow. A good example of this is when the person sits down and gets a great idea; it is the Elemental life which goes out (like a hunter) into the right domains to bring back what will further fuel the idea. This is allowing the inner and outer life to grow together, each nourishing the other

THE LIVING EVENT OF THE HUMAN LIFE

Problems arise in the person when the **Elemental life** of them is trained exclusively to cultural roles which do not bring the right kind of nourishment back to the inner life (CORE BEING). This results in a malnourished core and drives the person further away from their **original Entity of Self.** The proposition of the emancipation of self is the greater promise of being human and is unlikely to occur if the elemental side of them is waylaid and highjacked by cultural roles.

Sometimes one aspect of a person's core instinctively or intuitively feels that they need to re-balance themselves against a greater criteria and it is these feelings which will drive them out into Nature, to the forests, the mountains, the rivers or whatever. The **Being** life will be driven towards the need to refine, to heal and to take stock of self. It might be examining its own accountability. The **Elemental** side of the person will be drawn to anything elemental within the natural domain; it is likely the Elemental aspect of self that drives people to climb mountains or pit themselves against the dynamic power of the ocean. When William Wordsworth wrote "come forth into the light of things" and "let Nature be your teacher", ("The Tables Turned")[1] he was doubtless referring to both aspects of living.

---

[1] Lyrical Ballads, with a Few Other Poems. by William Wordsworth and Samuel Taylor Coleridge. 1798

APPENDIX Ii

GLOSSARY

Astral: the electro-magnetic domains of the Planet which contain everything that pertains to the Planet as well as a record of everything that has ever happened here.

Aura: the electro-magnetic field that surrounds a person or any living thing, that reflects inner process at whatever level it issues from.

Awake: the natural state of planetary life form and the Planet herself. Currently subdued in the majority of humans, hence the need to wake-up in order to re-engage with planetary and creational purpose.

Being: the inner life of a human being and part of the original entity of self, donated by the Planet herself.

Core: the Entity of Self in its original shape and form, as issued by the creational spawning. The WHAT of you as opposed to the who.

Culture: the organisation of human affairs for a collective purpose, including the necessary codes of behaviour, laws and governances essential for its enforcement. The purpose may be social, economic, religious, anything, or a conglomerate of many things. In the case of the current world culture, we have a media culture whose mission is primarily economic growth. Purpose is the operative word where culture is concerned as it pegs the level immediately.

Divinatory: the ability to read and interpret the unseen forces and frequencies emanating from a person or anything living, including places and times. Can stretch from clairvoyance to mediumship to empathy to sensitivity to psyche.

THE LIVING EVENT OF THE HUMAN LIFE

Divining: the ability to reach beyond the planetary and give shape and form to higher than planetary issue.

Earth Life: electro-magnetic life form doing duty on the Planet and commonly and colloquially known as fairies, elves, gnomes, sylphs, undines etc.

Elemental: (1) electro-magnetic life forms that are cone-shaped and are part of the maintenance system of planet Earth. (2) the outward expression of a human being.

Esoteric: knowledge and understanding contained in symbols, shapes and structures that pertain to how the planet and Creation works.

Head life: the higher possibility of the brain, currently dormant.

Law of Two: fundamental planetary law commonly thought of as the appearance of opposites eg up/down, life/death, hot/cold etc.

Law of Four: the natural cycles that govern the planet upon which we live and all life thereupon.

Laws: the indelible and permanent criteria that govern the structure of creation itself and all life form thereupon.

Life: that which exists to serve Creation and its purposes. It takes on form and shape in accordance with Creational need at whatever level it finds itself.

Occult: the natural power of life itself issuing through living form for example, the power that drives Spring and can cause a seed to push through concrete to reach the light, is highly occult.

APPENDIX Ii

Pentagram: a five-pointed star of sun level origin. The human is a living example of this.

Planetary: everything that occurs on the planet and is endorsed by her.

Roles: the many parts a person needs to play in order to survive in the culture they find themselves living in.

Solar: the entire solar system including the planets and the Sun itself; may be likened to a single cell within the body of Creation itself.

Sun level: the nucleus of the solar system without which the planet could not support and maintain life. A higher level than planetary.

Way: the natural pathway a person needs to tread in order to recover their original self and re-engage with planetary and creational purpose.

THE LIVING EVENT OF HUMAN LIFE

The origins of Creational Structure; the need for Life to live, serve and maintain it; Creational Law and the significance of the Law of Three; the beginning of life (the Spawning); the Entity of Self; the actuality of life at planetary level. The situation prior to actual conception: the gathering of Alive; the winning edge of impossibility (the enormous odds against a successful physical appearance); Cultural influence (the situation now); the Natural Laws (the fatality of Life at Planetary level).

The impact of time, human origins, Antiquity and the modern world; locating oneself on the Planet; the Entity of Self or individuality versus the collective; The considerations of Place and Form (in which we explore the Actuality of Life Upon the Planet); the considerations of the "as What": the True Entity of Self offset to the Human Historical Inheritance; Something else (Lack of Perfection impacting on the Design); the Collective (the Altogether as a Single Entity and Mind).

Conception to birth; the situation event; the transient attendances; other connections; the quickening and further development of the physical body; the Truth and Passion of Life itself; the 'Rite to Be'; lost Creational event; the 'Newbie'; initiation of being human; the installation of Being Elemental; the Occultism of the Alive to Life.

The passage to reincarnation; the greater human-made life; Awakened life without Human Identity; the Reborn life (in which Content replaces Entity of Self; the Transient Lines (in which Transience conflicts with Culture); the Abandonment of Entity for Identity; End results.

The second physical appearance on Earth. This includes the strong sense and recall of the first life; the Reborn life (a life of containment rather than re-connection to the Entity of Self); Elemental and Earth Life involvement; developing a pedigree or caste of Content.

The after-life stage prior to the third physical life; the considerations of Reincarnation; Transformation (where change itself changes the rules); further considerations of Reborn; Activity outside of settings.

APPENDIX Ii

The Continuous Revolution; new Difficulty of Self–unsettlement of the Inner Life; Entity Identity, Elemental and Earth Life; the considerations of the Way of the New Genius (Mental Inner Life Development and Self-Maintenance); the considerations of Greater Order and Criteria.

The situation prior to the fourth physical life; the second reincarnation/multiple life returns; the Pitching life; cocoons and sleepers; Earth life and Elemental involvement; considerations of reborn again; resurrection and the ascensional living event.

Life beyond the planetary; the Thereafter life; Resurrection; the Occult and the Esoteric; Alien interference in the Human Affair; Living or Serving Life; the Maintenance

THE LIVING EVENT OF THE HUMAN LIFE

COMING SPRING 2024

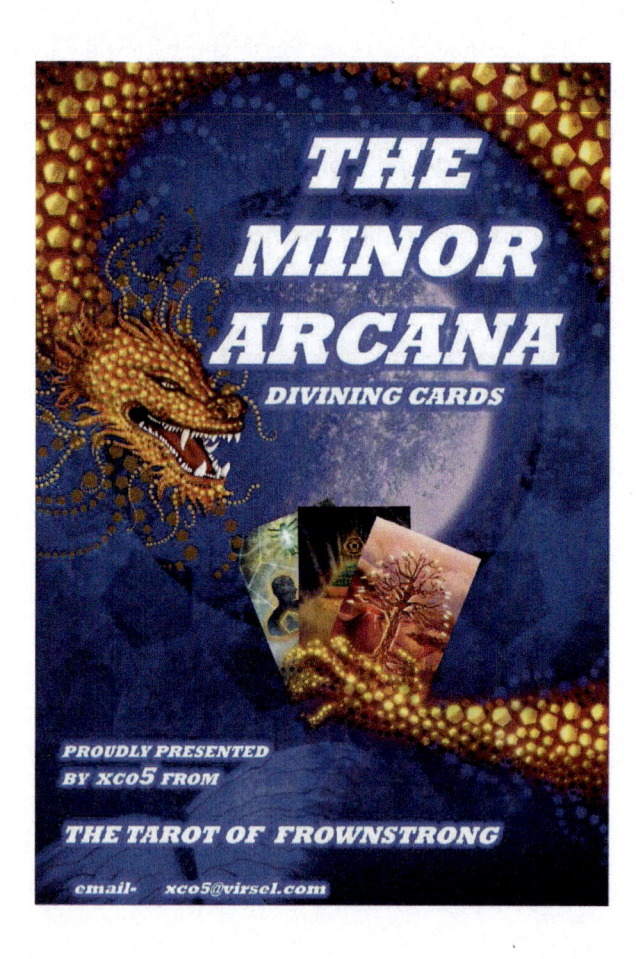

Created by the originator of Tarot of Frown Strong (aka Frownstrong Tarot, Tarot of Virsel) we will be publishing the support deck to run alongside and integrate with this highly prized deck.